The Artist's Journey:

The Perfumed Pilgrim Tackles the Camino de Santiago

Marcia Shaver

BOOK PUBLISHERS NETWORK

Book Publishers Network
P.O. Box 2256
Bothell • WA • 98041
PH • 425-483-3040
www.bookpublishersnetwork.com

10 9 8 7 6 5 4 3 2 1

Printed in the United States of America

LCCN 2010924095
ISBN10 1-935359-29-0
ISBN13 978-1-935359-29-6

Editor: Julie Scandora
Cover Designer: Laura Zugzda
Portrait Photographer: Joy Fischer (joyfischermemories.com)
Typographer: Stephanie Martindale

For my husband, Craig, who helped make this journey possible.

For Tannis, the perfect walking partner.

And for all the women out there who dream of adventure!

Buen Camino!

Marcia Shaver

Travel lightly,
You are not traveling for people to see you.
Travel expectantly,
Every place you visit is like a surprise package to be opened;
Untie the strings with an expectation of high adventure.
Travel humbly,
Visit people and places with reverence and respect for their traditions and way of life.
Travel with an open mind,
Leave your prejudices at home.
Travel with curiosity,
It is not how far you go,
But how deeply you go that mines the gold of experience.

~Spanish Proverb

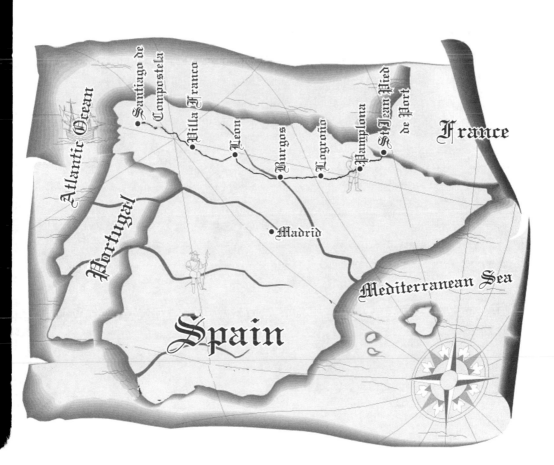

Early spring in the courtyard at Hospital de Órbigo

Contents

Introduction

When does a woman become invisible? As you give of yourself, does the color gradually seep out of your very being? Does all that unrecognized love and unpaid labor render you lighter and lighter until one day you look into the mirror only to see a faded image of the former you? Have you truly vanished, or does it just seem that people look right through you?

And how does it happen? Does a single event trigger the change? Especially demanding circumstances—physically and emotionally—have a way of extracting the juiciness out of your soul, as surely as if you had been pushed through the sieve. But the little day-to-day trials add to the transformation. I wondered, where had the soul of my soul gone?

Their comments tell all. And, yes, they hurt. Someone you care about patronizingly says, "You're really nice, but ..." Or you overhear the classic, "She hasn't worked for twenty years ..." You feel stabs of pain in realizing that people no longer think you are smart or value the work that you do. And, in some ways, you slip into thinking of yourself in the same way and feel you must prove the others wrong.

At some point, a woman finally understands that she must reclaim the power she willingly gave away little by little. She decides she will no longer let others define her. She will no longer limit her capabilities. With a growing sense of who she really is, she begins to set aside her fears, harnesses the dormant fire within her heart, and ventures into areas she never would have considered before. She challenges herself—not to prove anything to anyone, not even herself, but merely because *she knows she can.*

I had reached that point and longed for at least one epic adventure in my lifetime and felt a narrowing window of opportunity. I inhabited a reasonably fit body in these years after child-raising and had not yet needed to care for aging parents, so the time seemed right to set off in search of the person I once was. I was raised on the lore of my not too distant ancestors who put on their boots and walked two thousand miles to an unknown future through the wilderness on the Oregon Trail. Who were those brave and hardy souls who made up my gene pool and fired my imagination? For many, the journey began long before the start of the trail. One teenage forefather traveled from Switzerland to America, saw the country's promise, and returned home to bring his younger brother all the way to Oregon. I wear the face of Europe: Swiss, German, French, Dutch, English, Welsh, Scot. Yet, at my core I am a child of the American West: self sufficient, independent, comfortable with solitude and wide open landscapes, intrigued by challenges to be met and distances to be traveled. I had not had a backpack on in thirty years, but I heard the call to lace up my boots and walk across a foreign country.

The Way of St. James, also known as the Camino de Santiago, was one of the three major ancient pilgrimage routes in Medieval Europe, most popular from 1000 to 1300. In earlier times, pilgrims began their journey wherever they lived throughout Europe, and many routes converged in St. Jean Pied de Port, France, near the border with Spain. From there, the Camino stretches all the way to Santiago de Compostela in northwestern Spain, where St. James is buried. The classic section from St. Jean to Santiago is known as the Camino Frances and has a long history of notables who have walked it such as Charlemagne, St. Francis, King Ferdinand and Queen Isabella, El Cid, Napoleon, as well as countless less well-known souls. Before it became a Christian pilgrimage route, the Romans built a road "to the end of the earth" at Finisterre along this general path. Traveling ever westward, they followed the stars to the end of the known world where there was nothing left to see but the vast ocean stretching to what they believed was paradise. Earlier yet, the Celtic people had congregated in northwestern Spain, believing it was a place of great spiritual significance. They left huge stone dolmens and circular structures, reminding us of their vanished presence. Reaching back further into antiquity, fifteen thousand years ago, the first two-dimensional artists in Europe left the breathtaking painted caves known as the Sistine Chapel of Paleolithic Art at Altamira and throughout this region.

The journey is more important than the destination, and I hoped to let it unfold at a foot-traveler's pace in its unique way. The very act of walking so far, with the realities of one's life half a world away, would give me an opportunity for meditation and reflection concerning the intent with which I had lived. Spending so much time in intimate contact with the Earth especially appealed to me. I have always held a spiritual connection with the land, finding God in the miracle of the natural landscape. For me, it represents enduring beauty, strength, and eternity for it withstands the changes of time. Much like our hearts and souls, the landscape carries on, despite the onslaught of outside forces, evolving while staying the same. It is no accident that the symbol of the Camino is the scallop shell, linked to the Goddess Venus, who represents birth and regeneration.

Both excited and scared, I knew the way would present me with a huge challenge physically, emotionally, and spiritually. But I did not desire to go it alone; I sought a companion, one to travel over those bumps with me, to rejoice in the hurdles overcome, and to share in the transforming experience I hoped to gain. I felt confident my friend Tannis would be good company, walking through history on a spiritual journey, following in the well-traveled footsteps left by millions of souls over thousands of years. Traveling with open minds and innocent hearts, leaving our energy to mingle with the essence of all those who had walked before us, we would set out. We would follow the sun, west toward Santiago, through the varied and ever-changing landscape of Spain for five hundred miles and just let the timeless rhythm of the Camino create a unique experience.

Whatever would happen, I would have my epic journey.

Plaza San Marcos, León. Drawing by Tannis Moore

The Perfect Walking Partner

We are all travelers in the wilderness of this world,
And the best that we find in our travels is an honest friend.

Robert Louis Stevenson

I have to say I got really lucky. I had planned to walk the Camino with a good friend who had to cancel exactly two months before our departure date. So I asked my fellow artist, Tannis, to go along but I did not know her all that well. I realized that I had found a truly dependable and take-charge woman when she got physical therapy and a cortisone shot for a bum knee, renewed her passport, wrapped up all her projects, loaded her backpack, and bought her tickets in record time. What I did not know was how much fun she would be and how compatible we are in so many areas. I found not only the perfect walking partner; I discovered a friend for life.

I also found out that we have several characteristics in common that I never would have put on my priority list for the perfect walking partner. Tannis and I are about the same height and have a very similar walking stride. This is much more important than I ever dreamed. Several times we tried to walk with slightly taller people, and I was exhausted in half an hour. I was taking twice as many steps and felt as if I was almost jogging to keep up. Tannis and I are artists so we are very visual. We literally stopped to smell every flower, look at every rock wall, and take pictures continually. We never got impatient with each other because we were both grateful to have something beautiful or interesting pointed out that we might have otherwise missed. We were committed to the philosophy from the beginning to see the details and experience every possible moment as we moved through the countryside. We set our priorities to travel just far enough each day that we could still have the time and energy left to draw when we arrived. Watching other pilgrims rush toward their destination, covering too many kilometers and arriving exhausted without any idea of what they had just steamed past, baffled us. They missed so much.

When I was initially trying to lure Tannis into coming on the Camino with me, I had promised her wine and laughter every day. And I kept my word. We walked across an entire country, laughing away our cares instead of dwelling on the difficulties we had both been through recently. I do not mean to make our journey seem shallow because we did share confidences and hear each other's hearts speak. Giving voice to your concerns with uninhibited truth to someone who is listening with an open heart, no judgment, and not necessarily any advice unburdens and frees the soul. But true therapy comes from laughter. It banishes the least bit of anger or depression. And the more you laugh, the easier more laughter becomes. Sometimes we found ourselves walking in silence with a big silly smile on our face and nothing bad left in our minds. We did dorky things to entertain each other because nobody was watching. We made up jokes and fantasies about things we did not understand. We laughed until we had tears running down our faces about common things like the products offered in Spanish vending machines. I feel so blessed to have found Tannis, who created and shared this atmosphere of fun with the abandon of a child on holiday.

As I had suspected, the Camino physically challenged both of us. I could not have dreamed of anyone as supportive and caring in quiet ways. When my feet were swollen to the point of bursting sausages, Tannis massaged them, offered her socks to see if the thickness would be better, and carried the extra weight of the food for the day. When I felt like taking a taxi one day, she did not belittle me. Instead, she helped me see what that decision would mean for me from a different perspective in time. She just said, "I have been thinking about this situation in the opposite way. If you get in that taxi, you will regret it because it will be giving up. It is only five more miles, and I know we can make it." We walked on and I am really glad. That was the day that we instituted our no whining policy and a soul-cleansing substitute. We would say, in unison, "Uno, dos, tres, WAAAHHHHH!" This invariably sparked laughter and purged us of the need to feel sorry for ourselves.

The most important consideration in our compatibility was that we both had respect for each other. We knew beyond a doubt that neither of us would ask something unreasonable of the other one unless it was absolutely necessary. The Camino took on a fluid and timeless quality because we mutually decided each day how far we would walk with only the vague goal of twelve miles per day. Some days we stopped short of that, and some days we walked far further, but the final distance always came from a joint decision instead of a contest of wills. When I was weak, she was strong, and I hope the opposite was also true.

Thank you, Tannis, for helping to make this the journey of a lifetime.

Preparing for an Epic Journey

Once I discovered the pilgrimage route, I bought a pair of lightweight, waterproof hiking boots that would have left my ancestors who walked the Oregon Trail green with envy. I was then committed. As I began telling people what I was doing, so many "coincidences" happened. The young man at the bookstore had walked the Camino two years before and gave a lot of first-hand information and encouragement. I went to buy a backpack at the height of Christmas rush in downtown Seattle and grabbed the first clerk I ran into. It turned out he was from the province in Spain where the route ends, Galicia, and could tell me all about the weather, minimum and maximum temperatures, and so on. He had recommendations for the perfect sleeping bag, rain gear, and other essentials. What luck!

I made a big effort to learn Spanish, which is very difficult for a fifty-four-year-old brain. This time I did not trust my friends to help me. On a previous trip, I had asked my Portuguese friend how to say, "You are very handsome, but I am married." He taught me how to say, "I will do it for five bucks." As a result, I purchased a computer program and audiotapes. I worked on them almost every day for five months. At the end, I knew my skills remained very basic and I would talk like an infant, but at least I could try to connect with the people we would meet, whether they were villagers or fellow pilgrims. I also know that a smile, a helping hand, an attitude of gratitude and humility, or warm, friendly eyes can say far more than a correctly spoken sentence.

13th century church of St. Nicholas di Bari, Larrasoña

My physical training included working out at the gym, walking, horseback riding and a sensational downhill ski year. In evaluating equipment, I decided to opt for trekking poles to assist in the mountainous areas. Second-guessing my purchase, I wondered what kind of an uncoordinated person needed poles just to walk and determined to return them. Early the very next morning, I was walking the three miles home from the gym, listening to my Spanish lesson on my iPod. I was concentrating on saying with emphasis things like, "*Sí, señor!*"and "*Pantalones!*" So, one moment I was striding purposefully along, mumbling to myself in Spanish, and the next moment I found myself flat on my face on the pavement. I had had my hands in my pockets so I did not even catch myself or break my fall. Immediately a goose egg the size of a golf ball materialized on my forehead, and I had ripped open my elbow. Since I was lying on my hands and I was intensely in Spanish mode all I could say was "*No, señor, no entiendo!*" (No, sir, I don't understand.) I had no choice but get up and finish walking home, good training for the Camino. In the following days when I developed a really nice shiner of a black eye and a bruise on my elbow that extended four inches in each direction, I humbly realized what kind of an uncoordinated person needs poles just to walk. I guess you should never ask a question that you don't want an answer to.

I carefully considered what clothes and other equipment I would need as a minimum and purchased the lightest weight, fastest drying items available. I even bought the ultra-light panties making outrageous and unrealistic claims, along with the matching sports bras that give you the uni-boob look. For art materials I planned to take only a sketchbook, a pencil, and a couple of pens plus my journal. I even bought a new lighter-weight compact camera. I thought, *I am so good and I have planned so well.* In keeping with the "Survivor" theme, I bought a Buff as a multi-purpose clothing accessory, which can be worn as a scarf, a neck warmer, a mask, twelve different types of hat, or in any number of other creative ways. I allowed myself one luxury item: my two-ounce travel-size Chanel #5. I would not be the Pilgrim la Pew. A couple of weeks before departure, smugly confident that I was at about the fifteen-pound mark, I loaded my pack with everything I would be taking. I could hardly lift it. It weighed twenty-seven pounds. *EEEEEEKKKKKKK! How can this be? I am a backpack wimp, and I never would have agreed to this if I had known. Wahhh!* I was like the pioneer women who thought they could not leave Boston without the full set of china and the piano. Would anthropologists of the future find me petrified on the side of the trail, monumentally weighted down, wearing a two-ounce tee shirt, still clutching my Chanel #5? My fellow artist and Camino amiga, Tannis, came to my house with her pack of a similar weight, and we carefully went through every article to see what we could get rid of. It took three hours of careful evaluation and intense discussion. And we eliminated exactly eight ounces. Uh-oh! Were we in trouble!

To say I had pre-trip jitters and second thoughts about the wisdom of undertaking this journey is putting it mildly. At three days before departure, I had a nasty cold. All stressed out, I woke up that morning at 4:30. I had dreamed that I was practicing walking with my pack and it was so top heavy I fell over and could not get up. My husband, Craig, told me I was on my own because he would not be there to help me on the trip. As I groveled around and finally made it up, I got all dirty and thought I needed more clothes but could not possibly carry them. Soon after, I fell down again and realized Tannis had my hiking poles, which could have prevented my toppling over, but she was nowhere in sight because she was way ahead on one of her eleven-mile walks. Whimpering, I struggled to my knees then pulled myself the rest of the way up on a rock; meanwhile Craig was standing there with his arms crossed saying, "Tsk, tsk, tsk ..." That was so unlike him, and I was furious. (Aren't dreams retarded?) We crested a small hill, and I began to weave back and forth, frantically waving my arms for balance. You guessed it, I fell on my face again, and Craig pointed out that my pack was open and I should learn to secure it better because all my clothes had fallen out somewhere in the previous falls. I lay there knowing I could not get up again. I struggled really hard, but I was pinned by the weight of my pack. I woke up with twenty pounds of cat staring at me all slitty-eyed, demanding to know why his sleeping place was moving around and disturbing him so rudely.

Isn't this the way adventures go? You cannot plan for every eventuality or mishap, and you will always have some fear or reservation. If you are not falling down, you are not trying hard enough. All you can do is prepare as well as possible, face your fears, have a good laugh at yourself, and then put on your shoes and just walk forward, living your dreams.

Castillo San Carlos, Finisterre.

In the Beginning
March 30-31

After spending a week in Rome with my family, we made our way leisurely to the airport, only to find that the time was an hour later than we thought. What are the odds that all of Europe would change to daylight savings time the night before and not tell the tourists? We were met with gigantic lines and chaos, accompanied by much shouting and hand signaling in Italian. Obviously we were not the only ones to be clueless about the time change. Panic aside, I made my flight to Spain on time and then had five hours to kill in the Madrid airport. I got my first special treatment as a pilgrim when a nice Iberia Airlines employee tried to get me on a much earlier flight. He turned everyone else away, but quietly asked me to wait at the gate. Just as he was about to let me board, two people arrived at a run and claimed their reserved seats, filling the plane. He apologized, but I thanked him for trying and smiled.

When I arrived in Pamplona, the taxi driver thought I wanted to go to another town. Just as he was hitting the freeway, I said, "Pamplona Centro? Calle San Nicolas in Pamplona Antigua, near Plaza de Toros." This is baby talk in Spanish for, "The center of Pamplona? I need St. Nicolas Street in the old part of Pamplona, at the plaza near the bull ring." He was so astonished that I actually tried to communicate in Spanish that he whipped off the shoulder of the freeway, turned on the lights, got out his glasses, studied the address, and called his dispatcher. After a rapid conversation, he laughed and said dramatically, "*Tranquilla.*" At first I thought he was offering me a drink; then I realized the word meant "be calm" and had nothing to do with margaritas. We both laughed as he took the nearest roundabout at mach speed and headed back the way we had come. I found myself chattering away with him in basic Spanish and laughing together as we sped through the night. I was so proud of all the studying I had been doing. At the airport, he honestly reset the meter to zero and proceeded to my hotel. As he dropped me off, he gave me his card and told me if I needed anything or had any trouble at all to call him, patted my hand, and wished me a *buen Camino*.

In the darkness, I could see no street signs so I asked another man where my hotel was. He asked politely if I was walking the Camino de Santiago, and when I said yes, he escorted me to the door of the hotel, wished me a *buen viaggio* (good voyage), and blew me a kiss as he bowed. I couldn't believe it! What a wonderful welcome to Spain. I did not know if my special treatment was because I was a pilgrim, but three people had gone out of their way in the short span of a few hours to help me and be kind. I believed that boded well for our journey.

I checked into our very cute hotel expecting to see Tannis, who should have arrived before noon that day. But no Tannis. I checked my emergency cell phone for messages: Nada. I suspected that the time change had surprised her, too, thus making her miss her morning train. Because we were in a small hotel, the owners locked the doors at eleven, and the staff went home for the night. Tannis would not be able to get in. I decided to wait in the lobby—and had no choice but to share a table already filled with talkative French people who were smoking like chimneys. It was a wonder the fire alarms did not go off. The air was so thick with a blue fog of smoke that I could not see the front door. Just then, the ghostly image of a small woman with a big backpack materialized through the haze. Tannis! We were so glad to see each other that we squealed like sixth-grade girls and had a pajama party, talking way past midnight.

Pamplona, Spain, to St. Jean Pied de Port, France, via taxi
10,506 Steps, 4.5 Miles
March 31

The morning began at six thirty when I mumbled, "I slept like the dead. I could almost go back to sleep." I awoke two hours later in a puddle of drool. Our adventure had begun.

Wandering out to the nearest bar, we sucked down two super charged lattes, known in Spain as *café con leche*. Dark and rich, the aroma fills your senses with something close to heaven while simultaneously jump-starting your heart. As we sighed in contentment, our eyes met over the steaming cup of paradise, confessing that we were mutual caffeine addicts. That was the first of many shared joys.

The old section of Pamplona paraded its beauty as a light mist alternated with sunshine. The streets are so narrow that you can almost touch the buildings on each side with your arms outstretched. Tiny balconies of intricate ironwork overhang cobbled streets. Like a canyon, the winding streets focus your view on what is directly before you. Surprisingly, as you round a corner, huge elegant churches loom up to dominate the skyline, the stonework glowing a soft, warm yellow ochre against the porcelain blue backdrop of the sky.

We found the *refugio*, or pilgrim's hostel, and were met by a tiny, chain-smoking señora. Following a flurry of Spanish, she collected one euro each, issued our pilgrim's credential stamped with the wrong date, and sent us on our way. We found ourselves in the street within five minutes, laughing and wondering if the credentials were fake because they were so easy to get. We had read that you must declare your intentions and fill out volumes of paperwork. It appeared that the Spanish take a relaxed attitude toward the formalities.

We learned that it is not possible to get public transportation to St. Jean Pied de Port because you cross the border into France. Tannis and I agreed that dropping the first leg of our journey before we had even begun seemed like giving up. With a sense of anticipation, we bravely pooled our euros and got a taxi from Pamplona to St. Jean Pied de Port. We traveled through green hills full of sheep and horses, past cliffs, rivers, and gorges. The blue sky disappeared immediately, replaced by rain, turning to sleet and hail, as we gained elevation. Dread mixed with moments of panic as we passed many miserable looking pilgrims walking west through the cruel weather. In one hour, we traversed the distance it would take us nearly a week to walk on our return.

St. Jean is a magical little medieval town, cradled in the emerald embrace of the Pyrenees Mountains. The hills rise up steeply, shrouded in mist, giving way to mountaintops covered with snow. The town itself is all whitewash and mauve colored stone, red window shutters, narrow cobblestone streets, and flower boxes laden with blue, white, and deep yellow pansies. Bright pink cherry blossoms peeked over gray stone walls to frame the red tile roofs far below. It is here that the pilgrimage routes converge from Paris, Vézelay, and Le Puy to begin the Camino de Santiago across Spain. Its name literally means "Saint John at the foot of the pass."

Crowning the hill above St. Jean is the medieval citadel, whose massive gray stone walls have held the high ground to protect the city for centuries. Complete with double walls, arched gateways, and bridges, the citadel evokes a past when pilgrims and citizens faced a more hazardous and uncertain life. We descended the steep streets to the Church of Our Lady by the Bridge, built in the 1300s. Inside the cool, dark stone chapel, the stained glass cast colorful shafts of light. Soothing, celestial music floated through the candle-scented air as, contemplating the journey ahead, we asked for safe passage. We remained in a comforting meditation, reflecting on why we had come there and what we hope to discover.

After gathering euros, salami, bread, fruit, and chocolate for the upcoming days, we met a handsome Frenchman. He rattled off something long and seductive in French, which I interpreted as, "You are so beautiful I want to kiss you a thousand times!" It was certainly better than the alternative, "You women look like drowned rats." We tried for dinner but found only appetizers. So, I ask you, what is wrong with spending the afternoon in France, eating decadent chocolate crepes and drinking strong coffee? A lovely little restaurant with a red wooden deck overhanging the River Nive had enticed us. The sun broke through the clouds to illuminate the celadon green waters of the river passing quietly through town and under the Bridge of Our Lady. Satiated on café and chocolate crepes, we sat outside and drew for an hour until we were so frozen that our hands were shaking uncontrollably. We cracked the ice off and peered pathetically into the deserted room. The madame had locked us out on the deck, as the wind was blowing her doors open. Finally getting her attention, we returned to

"Bridge of Our Lady" over the River Nive, St. Jean Pied de Port, France

the fireside to continue drawing and await dinner. We were rewarded with a beautifully presented salad topped with hot bacon, garnished with walnuts, and accompanied by toast smothered in melting-hot goat cheese. Tender, flaky white fish in butter sauce followed the salad. It was melt-in-your-mouth delicious, washed down by a smooth local wine. That must be what heaven tastes like.

At nine o'clock, we returned to the refugio, all charged up to draw and write for another couple of hours, only to find everyone in bed with the lights out. Oops, major refugio faux pas on our first night! We stealthily crawled into our bunks and slept in all of our clothes, accompanied by our packs. I drifted off to sleep to a chorus of snores with a smile on my face.

St. Jean Pied de Port to Orisson
14,004 Steps, 6.0 Miles
April 1

This morning at O-dark–hundred, people got up and rustled around, making an incredible amount of noise while trying to be quiet. So much for returning the courtesy we showed last night. It was six thirty so we got up and found ourselves in a white-washed room with exposed pink stone framing the door and deep-set window. Heavy, dark ceiling beams above, tiled floor beneath, and about a dozen light-colored wood bunks within, the accommodations kept to the simple but clean and very pleasant. The communal dining area had two long trestle tables covered with vinyl cloths, an orange tabby cat, and a breakfast of coffee, bread, and apples. Our host, Jeanine Curutchet, was less than five feet tall, sporting red hair, a face full of character, twinkley brown eyes, and a contagious smile. Known as the Maman of the Pirigrinos, she gave us extra coffee and turned up the heat. She offered us ponchos and apples for the road. We stayed, writing in our journals, an hour after everyone else had gone. It was apparent that she was concerned we were lolly-gagging around too long to make the long hike to Roncesvalles, so we told her we were going only as far as Orisson. She laughed, clapping her hands, and smiling impishly. Raising her eyebrows, she informed us that Jean-Jacque, the proprietor of Orisson, was most handsome, adding a very French "huh huh huh!" On that note we saddled up, filled our water bottles from the fountain outside of her red door, and headed down the Rue de la Citadelle. Crossing the River Nive, we passed through the Port d'Espagne like thousands of pilgrims before us and left lovely St. Jean behind us.

We began walking up the hard way. Napoleon was insane! Like the Romans before him, in his invasion of Spain, Napoleon chose the high route over the top of the mountains because its openness discouraged sneak attacks by the enemy. We walked about fifty feet then pretended to look at the stone walls, when in reality we were embarrassed to admit that we could not breathe. Our hearts were pounding, and we were beginning to sweat in the cold morning fog. At the next stop twenty feet further up the road, we abandoned all pretense of pride as we stood leaning on our trekking poles and gasping for breath. Another thirty feet and we had to strip off our coats. It is amazing the heat you can generate in rain gear with twenty-seven extra pounds on your back, not to mention the extra twenty on my butt. Looking back to survey our progress, we found ourselves barely out of town! Our spiritual journey consisted of praying we would not keel over and die on the spot.

We pushed onward, pausing every hundred feet to rest. The green hills dropped steeply away into the mists and rain. Stone and white-washed houses with red tile roofs punctuate the verdant pastures with stone walls snaking over the steep contours. The tidy barns were filled with fat, content-looking animals. Yellow Scotch broom and a carpet of tiny wildflowers accentuated ancient, contorted, dark trees still bare of their leaves. Miniscule birds sang in the hedges, and the church bells tolled at noon, drifting on the clouds from St. Jean. The higher we climbed the rockier and steeper it became, rugged and mysterious in the swirling fog.

We saw a herd of sheep sporting dreadlocks, their bells ringing melodically. We continued past herds of plump cattle and sturdy look-ing horses. Soon we were completely encased in fog, and just when we thought it could not get any steeper, it did. Visibility was down to zero, and we noticed that by now even the sheep were wearing oxygen masks. With every leaden step, we fantasized what we could ditch out of our packs. Finally, we came around a bend, and there was our goal, Orisson Refugio. We had traveled only six miles, but the path had climbed straight up, and we felt proud we had made it. I was especially pleased that we had chosen this high, most difficult route on our first day.

The top was closed due to fog and snow, so the next day we would have to go by car back down to Valcarlos and lose all the elevation that we had gained that day. However, we definitely could have finished the Route Napoleon, one of the most challenging on the entire Camino, given the chance. Even though we would lose the elevation gain, I was proud that we attempted it. I felt optimistic that we might get a peek at the broader landscape the next morning. And the really good news was that I did not feel nearly as miserable as the pilgrims looked who we had passed the day before. It was kind of nice being out in the elements all day.

When we arrived at Orisson, a very chic madame showed us to a nice room with wooden bunks for eight people. We peeled off our wet clothes and hit the shower. Being an experienced marina person, I washed really fast, did my hair, then luxuriated in the remaining hot water (approximately ten seconds). Tannis, on the other hand, decided she needed to engage in a body scraping ritual by shaving her legs. When the water ceased with no warning, she was all soapy and had not rinsed her body or her hair. The madame had informed us we got only one token for the shower, so Tannis had no hope of continuing *la duche*. After some very un-pilgrim-like language, Tannis had to finish her shower in the sink while I attempted to get dry with my pathetically inadequate towel. This purchase claimed to absorb everything within a ten-foot radius and be suitable for industrial use. Hotels, car washes and restaurants would be thrilled with its fantastic qualities. Colorfast and lint free, its strength was Herculean. Yet, there I stood, damp and covered in a layer of orange fuzz. It struck me as very funny that the manufacturer must not think water is a chemical to be super absorbed.

Semi-clean and dry, we went to the common room to drink rich café au lait out of huge bowls and receive a steaming bowl of vegetable soup to warm up our salami and cheese lunch. We offered chocolate to everyone and made instant friends. Jean-Jacque, who was, indeed, very handsome, welcomed us with his sparkling eyes, an impish smile, and a hot, crackling fire. The fireplace, big enough to stand in, occupied the entire wall. A lace band hanging precariously near the flames softened the massive dark wooden mantle. Bright artwork accented the golden stone bricks and ivory walls. I suspected the deep-set windows opened out to a stunning view, but we were enveloped in a soft blanket of fog.

We sat at the long oak tables, drawing until dinnertime. Then came our feast—a beautiful and elegant meal of hot soup, homemade sausages, a vegetable dish, a lentil stew, scalloped potatoes, bread, and red wine. At the communal table, Tannis and I shared the meal with four French pilgrims and a bi-lingual French Canadian couple who served as translators.

Two of the French pilgrims, Yves and Francois, we had seen that morning at St. Jean. Francois was blind and his friend was guiding him. Yves walked first, providing a running commentary on everything they passed as well as physical support. Francois followed, holding on to the back of Yves's pack. They planned to walk all the way to Santiago. What a courageous and inspiring journey! In the coming days, we would see them walking steadily and cheerfully over the mountains, joined at the pack, talking quietly. It made me thankful for everything I *could* see, feeling less sorry for myself for missing the views of the Pyrenees. I would so much rather see mist and rain than nothing at all. Each thing we can see is a treasure and a gift.

A welcome fire at Albergue Orisson, France

Orisson to Roncesvalles
21,011 Steps, 9.01 Miles
April 2

This morning we checked Tannis's pedometer. The number of steps we had taken amazed us—from the time our feet had hit the floor yesterday when we got out of bed until we had dropped into our bunks at lights out. I certainly felt every step, and during the steepest parts, each one became a deliberate act of persistence. It is daunting to consider how many steps we may have ahead of us, and I wonder if we will be brave and strong enough to drag ourselves all the way across Spain. We have vowed that every step toward Santiago will count, regardless of whether we take it on the trail or around the village at our destination!

We were served a hot breakfast and coffee in BOWLS to fortify ourselves for our trek today. Now that is most civilized. But the outdoors had forgotten its manners. Thick fog blanketed the surrounding area and made the route over the top impassable. Jean-Jacque packed us into his car and roared down the mountain at breakneck speed. I sat white-knuckled in the front seat, applying the imaginary brakes, held fast by the g-force, praying we would not squirt right off the wet road and into the void. It was like riding a roller coaster in a whiteout. The tiny curving road had zero visibility, pitching straight down the mountainside. Amid my fears of flying off the road, I managed to wonder at the fact we had actually climbed that steep path the day before.

We began walking at Valcarlos, a tiny town in the bottom of a steep valley. Valcarlos means "valley of Charles," named after the Holy Roman Emperor Charlemagne. Unlike the Romans and Napoleon, Charlemagne chose the easy way out of Spain. Big mistake. In 778, the Basques nearly wiped out his army in this valley as he retreated from sacking Pamplona during his invasion of the country.

The way is a more gradual climb but continually up all day. We walked along the main road for a few kilometers. The bare trees had an almost purple tone against the green fields that they bordered. The rivers, high and powerful with all the spring rain, rushed through canyons and splashed over waterfalls. And above us, the jagged cliffs plunged dramatically downward, disappearing into the mists.

We found a pathway leading off the road and down to the river. At the bottom of the valley, we passed a group of stone barns and discovered that the road was washed out. Francois and Yves had to turn back, as fording the swollen stream was impossible for them. We sadly waved good-bye as they began retracing their steps back to the main road. Tannis and I tried to press on. We slogged up some muddy banks toward a log spanning the river that looked promising. Approaching it, I sank up to my ankles in the squishy goo and toppled forward, landing on my hands in the morass. Visualizing myself pinned down by my pack, unable to get up, and drowning with my face in the mud, I cringed at the embarrassment of dying such a messy death—and being remembered that way. Fueled by the ensuing adrenaline rush, I did a full-out push-up in the mud with a twenty-seven-pound pack on my back. The US Marines would have been proud! Once I recovered, we realized that the log was impossible to use as a bridge with our packs on. After further explorations, we had to concede that the river was too swift to cross. And even if we did get across the river, the banks on the other side were too steep and unstable to scale. Dejectedly, we turned back toward the main road.

Meanwhile, we both had to pee, so we observed proper etiquette and chose separate bushes. Not wanting to take off my pack, rain pants, regular pants and panties, I grabbed my handy accessory that allows women to pee standing up. I boldly and confidently stuffed it in my pants and proceeded to pee down my leg, into my pants and fill my boot. EEEKKK! I had just failed Freshette 101. What else could go wrong? (Wait, do they have bears in Spain?) I was now soaking wet and a mess on the outside from the rain and mud and on the inside from pee. Being a mom, I realized this was a set up for diaper rash, which can last for weeks. I squished over to Tannis and confessed, adding mournfully, "*Mis pantalones huele mal.*" (My pants smell bad.)

Despondently, we continued through ankle-deep mud. Past the barns, a short distance, we found we had missed the trail marker pointing up the hillside through the trees. How could we have missed it, as it consisted of several bright yellow arrows? If we had actually survived the river crossing, we would have been on the wrong mountain in the rain and fog, probably headed back toward the remote Route Napoleon. We could see the road across the creek ascending to nowhere, disappearing into the low clouds. At the least, we would have spent a very cold night alone on the mountain, and who knows if anyone would have even looked for us. Pilgrims do die every year on the Camino, many of hypothermia.

We ascended through beech forests, some of the last remaining natural ones in Europe. The ground was covered with heather, Scotch broom, and another beautiful yet spiky bush that scratched my exposed ankles and calves. But of course. After all, Roncesvalles does mean "valley of thorns." I was so tired. It is amazing how a series of small goals can get you such a long way. "I just have to make it to that next turn" or "that rock is as far as I have to think about" got us slowly but steadily up the mountain. We stopped to rest, then walked to the next tree or marker. It quickly became obvious that we had trained at sea level, on flat ground, without our packs. Climbing mountains hauling an extra twenty-seven pounds in inclement weather with mud oozing over the top of your boots and between your toes, wearing pants you had peed in, is slightly more difficult. We eventually found ourselves at Puerto Ibañeta where patches of snow, dense fog, and a cold, pervasive wind signaled the top. We sighted the church and were greeted by cheers of "You made it! You made it!" from Yves and Francois. We took shelter under the eves of the church near the monument to Roland, the French hero who died here in battle blowing his horn belatedly to alert the rest of Charlemagne's troops trapped in the valley below.

Encased in mist, we wound our way down through running streams in the trail and over tangled webs of roots covered in moss. The weather especially made the place feel very primal, much as it must have felt for the pilgrims who have passed this way for over a thousand years. A knight in shining armor on his valiant charger, emerging through the veil of time, would not have surprised us. The steely gray roof of the church and monastery at Roncesvalles was a welcome sight. Built in the early 1100s, it contains the bones of Charlemagne's fallen soldiers, including the legendary Roland, along with the bones of pilgrims who died trying to cross the Pyrenees. It was one of the earliest and most important places offering shelter to pilgrims walking the Camino.

The open-door philosophy of hospitality, which includes everyone, still exists today. The monastery itself is a huge gray stone structure with vaulted ceilings and approximately a hundred bunk beds. Looking at the depth of the windows, I guessed the walls were at least five feet thick. Just as Tannis was thinking of downloading her sleeping bag and mailing it to Santiago, we discovered the accommodations provided no blankets. She would have spent a cold and sleepless night. However, this place had everything else: two computers with Internet, a phone, hot tea, showers, and best of all, a friendly German volunteer who did our laundry! What a gift and a luxury we received from this angel of the clean clothes.

The sun came out as we sat on a stone wall and drew until the wind drove us back inside. The Gothic chapel of St. James constructed in the 1200s was my subject. Its gray weathered stones hold the bell, which once graced the chapel at the Ibañeta pass, a ringing beacon, guiding pilgrims through the prevailing mists.

We gratefully sat down to the pilgrims' dinner at Casa Sabina restaurant with Yves and Francois. It was a huge bowl of pasta, followed by a whole trout each, French fries, a bottle of red wine, and excellent yogurt, all for eight euros each. In almost every town along the Camino, the local bar offers a hearty and tasty pilgrim's menu for around eight to ten euros. This reasonable price generally includes a big salad, often with tuna, some type of meat or fish, bread, dessert, and either wine or water. Sometimes potatoes or pasta are included. What a treat to sit down at a communal table each night and have a delicious meal prepared by someone else!

Warm, dry, clean, and full of exquisite food, we went to the eight o'clock pilgrim's mass at the Iglesia de Santa Maria to partake in the communal blessing of our journey. We took the front row seats, forgetting about not knowing what to do with all the standing up and sitting down during the service since we are not Catholic. It didn't help that it was all in Spanish. Rats! We couldn't even watch everyone else on the

13th century Capilla de Santiago, or Chapel of St. James, Roncesvalles

sly since we were way up front. However, we did appreciate the beauty of the church with its heavy, carved gray stone columns and lovely stained glass windows. The acoustics allowed the voices to echo through the entire space and carried the soft voices of the priests as clearly as if they had been amplified by microphones. The candles, chanting, soft music, and fluid rhythm of the Spanish language combined to offer a mystical feeling, perfect for the religious setting.

Roncesvalles to Viskarret
21,014 Steps, 9 Miles
April 3

As I lay in bed, I thought about the hilarious scene surrounding me—people walking around in their underwear, scratching their butts. And I am not sure who to blame for the symphony of snores, but I think that is international.

We set out from Roncesvalles on tired legs but have no blisters yet. The gravel trails through the woods were gradual. We wound past dairy barns with new calves on unstable legs, then came upon a field full of small, stout, frisky horses, and stood watching them play. They looked positively prehistoric. They seemed to be a cross between a draft horse and a pony. Ponies on steroids! Yak ponies! What could they be? Many of them came to the fence, stretching their necks toward us in search of treats and pets. A large male butted in and tried to steal all the attention. Not to be intimidated, one of the smaller ones began biting his tail and pulling chunks out of it. They appeared to be smiling, adding to their unusual looks. Most were dark bay brown with black manes, tails, and stockings. Others were a rusty tan color with blond manes and tails. They had shaggy coats and short, thick, sturdy bodies. Their manes were so full that they covered half of their faces, giving them a mischievous, playful look. They resembled the horses featured in the cave paintings of this region. I believe they were Pottoks, or the native wild horses, believed to have been descendants of the Magdalenian horses of 14,000 to 7,000 BC. These horses have been an integral part

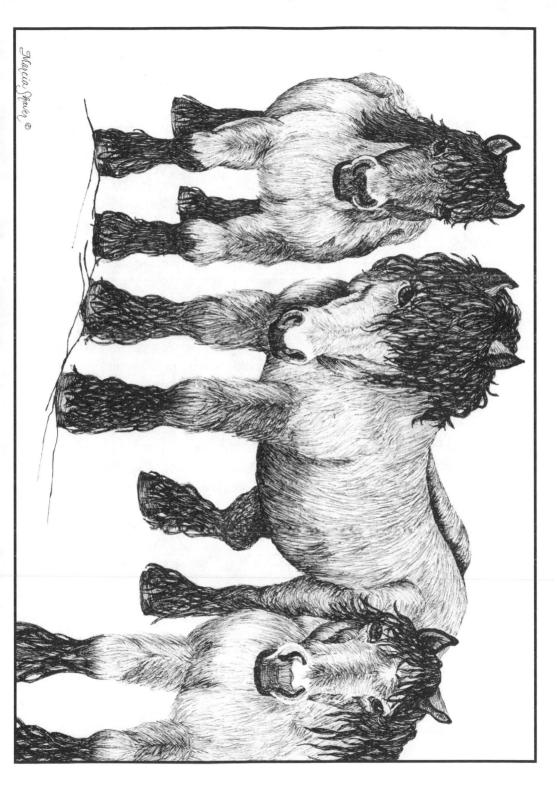

Basque horses of the Pyrenees mountains

of Basque life for centuries. Most are domesticated now, but until fairly recent times, some still ran wild in the mountains.

We continued through rich pastures, steep rolling hills, and beech forests. There were a multitude of clear streams crossed by simple foot-bridges made of huge, flat slabs of rock. They seemed to be growing organically right out of the streams. It was misty most of the morning, magical in its own way. Yellow primroses grew everywhere, the fields showed a startling green, and the trees were just beginning to bud and flower. The air smelled fresh, and ambling stone walls sometimes bordered the paths. Over the crest of a hill, we would glimpse small, whitewashed villages with red tile roofs tucked into the landscape. The skies cleared at midday and gave us a spectacular day to walk through the verdant Basque lands. It is no wonder that the landscape is so lush, as the average regional rainfall is fifty-eight inches. That is more than the western coast of Ireland gets and one and a half times as much as Seattle.

We stopped at the little town of Burguete, where Hemingway used to hang out and go fishing when he was not being chased by bulls in Pamplona. It is a lovely little Basque village with whitewashed buildings. The deep red shutters, doors, and balconies decorate the big houses, making them look more like Swiss chalets. We stopped for our first café con leche and the last two pastries in town near the austere gray church of St. Nicholas. In medieval times, the church and the town served the pilgrim trade much as it does today. It seems hard to believe that this quiet area was a haven in the Middle Ages for robbers preying on unsuspecting pilgrims.

After nine miles, we reached the tiny, ancient village of Viskarret and decided to stay at the Casa Rural Posada Nueva. We had a private room, and the señora keeps an immaculate house. The town of Viskarret is very small but tidy and has a Romanesque church. The solidly built whitewashed houses have exposed stone corners and big, steep overhanging red tile roofs to shed the plentiful rain and snowfall of the region. They have ornately carved roof supports and balconies, heavy doors, and shutters all painted a deep red. As we explored the town, searching for a drawing site, we met Carlos, an eighty-year-old, blue-eyed gentleman wearing a black beret and a big smile. His happiness was

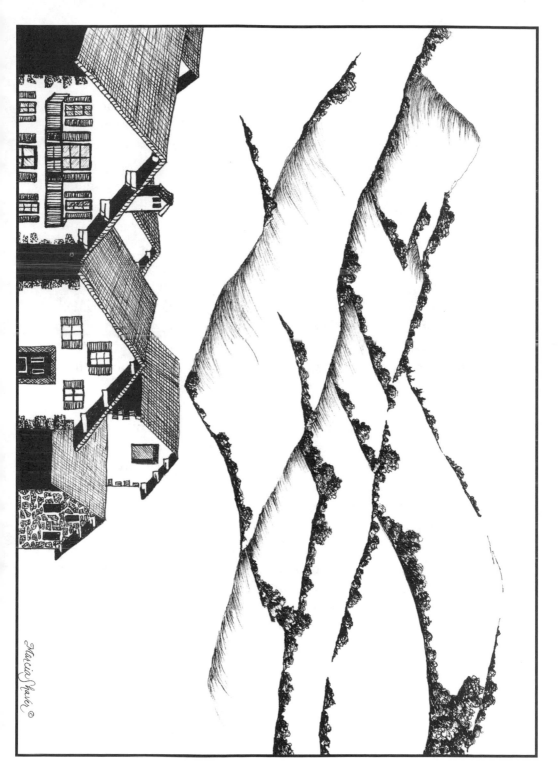

The village of Viskarret

contagious as he told us of his adventures walking the Camino many years ago. He now lives with his memories, two hip replacements, and a pair of crutches, yet his smile never faltered as he traversed the streets of his village. As the sun shown and the wind picked up, I thought what a good way he was living out his last years rather than being consigned to some nursing home.

After spending the afternoon drawing, we treated ourselves to the luxury of soaking in a near scalding bath. Our host, the tiny señora, prepared a fabulous dinner of pasta, fried cutlets, crisp salad, and fresh fruit served by her fireplace. We shared dinner with Reiner, a German, and Martien, a Dutch man. Martien is very easy to talk to and provided a bridge with Reiner due to his fluency in both English and German. If only all people could just talk to each other, we could avoid so many conflicts and misunderstandings in this world. It makes me sad that in America we place so little value on language study in our schools. We are missing such a rich opportunity to know others.

Martien was kindly helping Reiner treat the worst blisters I have ever seen. We had met Martien earlier at the café and shared our ibuprofen to help with his aching knee, encouraging him to stay in Viskarret and take an easy day. This scenario became a theme on the Camino: all the pilgrims helped each other with injuries, compared and exchanged drugs, and shared the sometimes amazing stories of trials and courage that had brought them here. This caring attention provided a simple yet intimate and powerful bonding process. I so wished the kindness and trust that flowed along the Camino, given freely and from so many diverse hearts, could be spread across the entire world.

Viskarret to Larrasoaña
30,021 Steps, 12.77 Miles
April 4

We went to sleep last night to the sounds of mad, passionate lovemaking from a German couple who had arrived late in the evening. At least we assumed that was what they were doing from the squeaking bed, the moving furniture, the laughter, and the loud, "yah, yah, yah" coming through the walls. They must have been on their honeymoon.

As we were departing after breakfast, the señora refused to let Reiner leave because he did not have enough money to pay for his room. There was no cash machine in this village, or for many miles. Tannis loaned him ten euros, and for quite some time he walked with us. We told him to go on at his own pace; we trusted him, and we would see him that night. It is such a bad feeling not being able to use a credit card, being out of cash, and not being able to get any more. Tannis and I philosophically discussed the fact that we might never see Reiner or the ten euros again and agreed to split the difference. We really did not know him, at all. However, he was waiting in Larrasoaña as promised, so our good faith was rewarded.

It was an absolutely flawless day. A clear, deep cobalt blue colored the sky, and the birds were singing. We were on pathways all day that wound up over forested ridges, then down through velvety fields. The trees flowered more each day, and wild flowers put on a bright display for miles—pink, yellow, white, and even periwinkle spots of color were sprinkled everywhere. Their perfumed fragrance filled the air. Although the trails were still very muddy, they felt firmer under foot, and my boots kept my feet dry. We ascended through twisted oaks that looked like a bonsai master had been at work trimming them, silhouetted against the intensely blue sky, then entered a forest of sweet smelling pines. Near the pass was the ruin of an ancient pilgrim's hostal where I successfully passed Freshette 101 and received the distinguished award of dry pants. I felt very brave and coordinated for attempting it again after such disastrous results the first time! Once I mastered planting my feet widely, tucking in my butt, and peeing standing up like a man, I didn't care if I ever did it again. These are such small victories to feel good about.

As we were approaching the summit of the Alto de Erro, we saw *huge* birds circling and floating on the wind currents. They were the griffon vultures, three and a half feet long with wingspans of nine feet. They are beautiful dark-colored birds with a white head and neck ruff, and a bright yellow bill. One of the biggest birds living in the wild in

Europe, the griffon vultures live on rocky ledges and crags and lay only one egg per year. In recent years, they have not been finding enough to eat because the E.U. passed a law that any animal remains must be removed from the fields quickly. Normally they feed on carrion, but lately they are so hungry they have taken to attacking live prey. Although we may have smelled like we were dead, we were not quite there yet, so we picked up the pace to discourage them from swooping down and picking us off for their lunch.

At the pass, we stopped to eat our lunch in the sunshine. Tannis shared the story of her journey this year into the uncharted waters of parentlessness. Without a compass, sailing alone on that slick surface of newly found uncertainty must feel disorienting and frightening. Losing both her mother and father so quickly in succession was devastating. My heart ached as I heard her tale of bravery and loss. High in the Spanish mountains was a good place to set the memory of her parents free on the winds.

As we somberly descended the steep pathway toward Zubiri, a smiling little border-collie-type dog appeared to accompany us like a spirit guide. He trotted ahead on the trail, exploring every rock and tree, and then continuously circled back to meet us again. He lifted our spirits and distracted us from thinking too deeply about Tannis's loss. It was a gentle easing from sadness back into beauty, and we were profoundly grateful. In honor of our pilgrimage, we named him Santiago. He entertained us and kept our company all the way into the local park in Zubiri. As we ate our snacks, he played fetch with abandon. Soon the local children were playing with him as well. The woman at the refugio was concerned that he was a lost dog because a pilgrim had seen him at Roncesvalles earlier in the week. He had a collar but no ID tags, which caused much discussion, and ended with a call to the police. Soon three tall, burly, darkly handsome, machine-gun-toting, Guardia Civil arrived in full battle uniform. There was a hugely dramatic discussion involving the Guardia Civil and half the village, puzzling over what to do about a cute little stray dog. Eventually the Guardia Civil went to have coffee with the attractive refugio volunteer, the villagers went home, and we left Santiago happily playing in the park with the

"Santiago" the spirit guide

local children. Problem solved Spanish style! Living on the Camino is not a bad life for a dog. He certainly did not look hungry or starved for affection, and he made us happy.

We crossed back over the River Arga on the medieval Puente de la Rabia, or "bridge of rabies." It was once believed that driving any animal under the bridge would cure it of rabies. It is a wonder that the entire population of humans and animals were not infected with horrible diseases if they promoted cures like that. A short distance later we passed through the middle of an active, modern mining operation. Aside from the ugly heaps of minerals and rock, we marveled at the fact that we could just walk right through private industrial land with not so much as a fence. Apparently the Camino was here first, and Spain deems it more important than the mining corporation. I like that value system.

Larrasoaña was an important pilgrim's stop in the eleventh century and beyond. Today it is a one-street village with very large whitewashed houses. The balconies and roof supports are beautifully carved dark wood, featuring flowers, animals, faces, and the names of the occupants. Several houses feature coats of arms, denoting the wealthy families who have lived there. One house had a huge ancient rose climbing up two stories, intricate lace curtains, and many pots holding early spring flowers. It was obviously a well loved and cared for home. The doors opening on to the streets are heavy and have a section that opens independently, revealing dim interior courtyards.

Near one of the houses, we met a man feeding his flock of fat reddish brown chickens. He had one *huge,* macho rooster, which he seemed very proud of. The rooster strutted and puffed out his chest, as if to say, "I'm the big guy in town, so all you hens just bow down!" We laughed and had a pleasant exchange with the man, including pantomimes of his rooster. In one small walled off area between buildings, he kept a flock of chickens that probably supplied the entire village with eggs and meat. He fed them table scraps and yesterday's bread, using the manure to fertilize his garden. It was the ultimate in efficiency and recycling.

We spent a quiet afternoon drawing on the fourteenth-century bridge spanning the Río Arga. The river was running strongly beneath

The proudest rooster in Larrasoaña

us, and curious, bright green lizards darting across the stones surrounded me. I drew the thirteenth century church of St. Nicolas di Bari, which stands at the head of this small town. It has maintained its hospitality, offering shelter to pilgrims, for centuries. It once boasted an Augustinian monastery, two pilgrims' hospices, and the brotherhoods to support them.

We had kept pace with Martien and Reiner today, so we shared another companionable dinner with them at the local bar. The nations represented at the communal table were France, England, Germany, Holland, America, and Spain. You get to meet interesting company and have enlightening conversations at such international gatherings. I sat with Mark and Andy, two Brits from Manchester. They were walking the Camino for one week, then returning next year to continue where they will have left off. Many Europeans walk the Camino this way, and I admire their tenacity in returning year after year. In many ways they are probably able to absorb each section in more depth with a year in between to think about what they have seen and what is in the upcoming regions. We talked about our homes, and I showed them some pictures of my family and the Pacific Northwest landscape. Mark said, "Good God, *this* is where you live? It is absolutely stunning! *What* are you doing in Spain?" I believe it is impossible for Europeans to grasp the sheer vastness of the unsettled American and Canadian West. I doubt that they even have a word for "wilderness" as we know it, those places that perhaps no person has ever set foot on, let alone the understanding that you can walk for hundreds of miles without coming across a town. The fact that we still have virgin forests and active volcanoes, as well as huge tracts of land with absolutely no civilization that are larger than some of the European countries, is difficult to explain without sounding arrogant.

However, we do not have anything like the Camino where you can meet people from all over the world and share this spiritual and physical journey. We do not have Santiago, and all that it represents. I felt at a loss to explain adequately what I admired on this journey within the context of where I came from, so I put my pictures away and did not bring them out again for the rest of my time in Spain. I had not anticipated such a reaction when I had brought them along with a map of America, Washington State, and the latitude comparison to Europe. I had wanted to say in pictures, "Look, I live at the same latitude as Paris, so we have cold, short winter days and beautiful summers. My state is about half the size of Spain and has similar diversity in landscape and climate. We have much in common." It is no wonder that we have trouble communicating with the rest of the world if I cannot even properly explain something as basic as that to someone who speaks my own language.

Larrasoaña to Pamplona
29,700 Steps, 12.6 Miles
April 5

We were awakened at five thirty by rustling plastic bags. For crying out loud, it did not even get light for two hours. We had no breakfast and NO COFFEE! It was quite remiss of us not to have planned better. We were practically the last ones out of the hostel, or *albergue* (al-BER-gay), setting out around seven thirty. Our walk began with the rising light. The sparkling, crystal frost was heavy on the trees and pastures, disappearing gradually as the sun warmed the day. Traversing the hills above the valley, we looked down through wild boxwood, the colors ranging from green through yellow ochre, to a reddish burnt sienna. Below us lay well-tended land and neat kitchen gardens filled with new spring greens, garlic, and onions. Spring was gradually unfurling herself before our eyes, showing her abundance everywhere we looked.

We paused at a pasture full of pregnant mares and one brand-new colt, still wobbly on his newfound legs. We watched him for quite some time trying to nurse, leaning against his mother, and sniffing things. He was just hours old, the steam rising off his coat, a new arrival to our world. What a miracle.

The terrain changed from mountains to hills and finally to a broader, more open landscape. We saw intriguing deep purple wildflowers that resembled little cactus formations. They emerged from the solid rock of the trail, delicate yet intensely sturdy at the same time. Vivid yellowish green, waxy succulents with purple flowers hung over banks and rocks with an impossibly long reach. In the early morning sun, we passed fertile farms, men fishing in crystalline streams, and contented dogs. We were following the Río Arga, which was running swift and full. The water had a pearly gray-green opaque look reminiscent of glacial melt. The lyrical sounds of the river provided a soothing background to bird song and the crunch of our boots on the gravel. The scent of pine drifted on the air, alternating with the smell of animals and freshly turned earth. Deer bounded through the fields, and large birds soared overhead. The sun kissed our cheeks with the first sunburns of the year. I felt myself getting stronger every day and the cares of the world diminishing with each step we took. Walking through the countryside, having no contact with the outside world, was soothing to my mind and my soul. Gradually the worry and stress simply slipped away unnoticed. In its place, a profound sense of peace settled in, which left room for the new and unexpected.

We passed through one beautiful village and then another with no bars or cafés in sight. By the time we reached Trinidad de Arre, it was noon, and we were famished. You would have thought we were about to perish although we could hardly have called our pilgrim dinners light fare. As we entered town, two Italian pilgrims stealthily approached us. I should have known better! A conversation with my friend, Mario, a few years ago had set me straight. I had complained after a recent visit to Italy that the men in the north seemed to have been to reform school since I had last been there. He candidly replied, "You should have more fun in the south, and if the men fail in their duty as Italians, come on over when you get home. I will make up for the shortcomings of my countrymen."

All that I had forgotten. It is amazing how you can only focus on one thing when you are drop-dead hungry. Your good judgment simply abandons you. They offered us oranges and smiles. We made the mistake of smiling back. You could practically taste their self-confidence, and it was obvious that the possibility of rejection was out of the question. When they seductively said, "The Americana women are very beautiful," did we run the other way? NO! I was all relaxed from strolling through the mountains, smelling the flowers. I said, "Grazie, grazie," and accepted the orange, forbidden fruit that it was. A simmering pout and raised eyebrows followed. He proceeded to tell us that it was the first job of Italians to love. Jeez, pick up lines must be their national sport. An instant vision filled my head of handsome, sensuous Italian men on an assembly line, working diligently to see how many pieces of a middle-aged woman's broken ego they could fit together into a completed female who felt beautiful and desired. Naturally, as soon as they finished with one woman, another one would follow. Their work would never end, and they would die happy yet exhausted. Did I throw the orange at him? NO! In my hunger-crazed state, I just drooled and said, "Oh, you Italians." He interpreted the drooling as a sign that we were hot for him, blew us a kiss, and then asked for a real one. Did I clamp my mouth shut and run with the orange? NO! I innocently went to give him a kiss on the cheek and got one full on the mouth. What was I thinking? "Mi scusi, signor, I can see from your skillful removal of my tonsils that you must be a surgeon. I sort of need them back though," I replied with a blush. Even though we were dizzy with hunger, we ignored their genuinely wounded, puppy-dog looks and pleading to join them for breakfast. I was too hungry to entertain the possibility that they would eat my breakfast right out of my mouth. We forged on past the café where they stopped, and pounced on the nearest smoke filled bar. We inhaled two café con leches and huge omelets each without even breathing.

After five days in the mountains, we had entered suburban Pamplona. Tiled buildings and clean streets gently introduced us to the city as we made our way through the first traffic we had seen in almost a week. The wide boulevard was lined with plane trees, whose branches had been woven together across the sidewalks to form a running archway. They provided a canopy of welcome shade in the summer, and for us in this early spring, they formed intricate graphic shapes in white and gray against the deep blue sky, organically twisted and braided.

We lost our markings and were looking confused, consulting the guidebook. A tiny lady sunning herself on a nearby bench motioned us over to her. She directed us in *rapido* Spanish with flamboyant hand signals for a full five minutes while we nodded and smiled. We could not understand a word she said. However, in a bold act of faith, we set off in what seemed entirely the wrong direction. We could hardly refuse to go the way she had pointed after all that help. We glanced back, and she was happily cackling on her bench, strategically placed at the busy intersection. We wondered briefly if she just sat there lying in wait for hapless pilgrims, sending them the wrong way back to France. Would she sit there, getting her entertainment for the day visualizing us staggering back over the Pyrenees? We soon found a scallop shell sign and knew that she really had helped us. We felt momentarily ashamed for having been so suspicious, but it was much too beautiful a day to worry.

We checked into the immaculately clean Casa Paderborn, sitting on the bank of the Río Arga, which is run by a German confraternity. We felt pampered beyond measure to have a room with only four women, a hot shower, and the opportunity to explore the lovely city of Pamplona on a sunny afternoon. The albergues, or refugios, are situated every few miles along the entire Camino. They are run by churches, towns, various pilgrim confraternaties, or private individuals. Similar to youth hostels, they provide a place to sleep, usually in bunk beds, a communal area in which to relax, basic services such as showers and toilets, and sometimes they also feature a kitchen. All of the facilities are co-ed, which generally includes the bathrooms and sleeping areas. The price ranged from a donation to about twelve euros, with the most common fee at eight euros per person. Only open to those with a pilgrim's credential, which you obtain at the beginning of your journey, they provide an inexpensive and safe place to stay along the way as well as a meeting place for people from all over the world. The albergues in Spain do not take reservations, so space is allotted on a first-come first-serve basis. We were never turned away from an already full albergue, and the lack of ability to plan added to the timelessness of the Camino experience. Of course, there are private hotels along the way as well, but I felt that we would miss a very important element of our passage along the Camino if we did not meet and bond with the international band of pilgrims bound for Santiago.

We crossed the lovely medieval bridge, the Puente de Magdalena, with the Pamplona Cathedral dominating the skyline. The cathedral was begun at the end of the fourteenth century on the site of an earlier Romanesque church that collapsed in 1390. The current façade was added in the late 1700s and projects a strong and forbidding feeling. In contrast, the interior contains alabaster tombs that are both light and delicate. Many of the kings of Navarre were crowned within this very cathedral.

The old city walls stand in a double formation with a large park-like strip in between that we assumed was a moat in earlier times. The massive inner rock walls date to the 1500s and must be seventy feet tall in places. We passed through a medieval stone arch topped by a crest featuring double eagle heads. The heavy chains, ballast stones, and the working mechanisms for the drawbridge are still in place. This is the Portal de Zumalacarregi, or the Portal de Francia, through which pilgrims and other travelers have entered Pamplona from France for hundreds of years. The ascent into the city is daunting, and I understand the powerful intimidation visitors from a more dangerous past would have felt when approaching this fortress. To have successfully mounted an attack against these formidable walls must have been impossible. This was an originally Basque village from a time long before the Romans arrived in 74-75 BC to establish a settlement under the general Pompaelo. Their baths, forum, houses, and markets once occupied the area where the cathedral now stands. The far-reaching influence of the Roman Empire is astonishing when you consider that even today Pamplona is the Spanish name derived from the founding Roman general. The Basques were there first, the Romans occupied the site for roughly four hundred years, then it was ruled under the Visigoths, the Moors, the Franks, the kings of Navarre, and later a unified Spain. Yet it is the Roman name that has stood through time.

Inside, the old city has many narrow cobbled streets leading into pleasant little plazas. We were treated to a Basque folk life festival with beautiful children dressed in authentic costumes of the region. Music and dancing, traditional games, and food vendors in the streets created a party atmosphere, lively and colorful. The tapas bars did a brisk

The medieval bridge "Puente de la Magdalena" over the río Arga, and
Pamplona's Cathedral, begun in 1394

business while the parade of a glorious Spanish afternoon circulated through the Plaza del Castillo, the heart of the old city. Surrounded by fathers with soccer balls and little boys, teenagers out to be seen looking fantastic, grandparents with little ones in strollers or on roller blades, handsome Guardia Civil, ice cream and fine wine, we sat writing in our journals on a bench. Several men joined us momentarily, then smiled and moved on. One particularly persistent older man kept talking in Spanish that I could sort of understand. When he said he was an official cantor for the Fiesta San Fermin, I brightly told him that my son and I had attended the fiesta, known to the rest of the world as the Running of the Bulls, a few years ago. He introduced himself as Salvatore, and asked me to go away with him in his car and drink wine to my heart's content. I told him I was married. He said I had a beautiful face. I smiled. He began to sing the songs of San Fermin to me, in quite a nice voice. By now he was holding my hand and people were starting to watch the show. I said "Bravo!" after the impromptu concert, and he stroked my hand and arm, telling me I must be a princess and do no work because my hands were so soft. Then came a long and soulful story about a mother in Cuba for fifty years, and a dead wife, followed by the news that he was free to entertain me at his casa, which was muy grande by the way.

"Uh-oh, ah, no entiendo senior," I shyly answered, while trying to retrieve my hand. ("I don't understand, sir," which was, of course, a total lie.) "Sí, sí, I could show you paradise," he countered, beginning to feel my leg. "*I am a pilgrim*, and I am on a spiritual journey to Santiago," I replied in the most holy voice I could muster while trying not to burst out laughing. "Sí, sí, I can see you are a most worthy señora of great character. But why walk all that way to Santiago when we can go in my car and have a fiesta muy magnifico? We could make beautiful music together." I darted my eyes at Tannis, who had been looking on in fascination. Like a good ventriloquist, I said, without moving my smile, "Help! Make a big deal of leaving and I will follow!"

We made our final escape and left him looking heartbroken on the bench in the sunshine. First the Italians, then Salvatore … I am a goddess!

Pamplona to Uterga
30,824 Steps, 13.13 Miles
April 6

We parted company with Martien and were quite sad. We had become accustomed to his quirky personality, his kindness, and his constant presence. We had not seen Yves and Francois for a few days. Once you get off cycle with people, you don't usually see them again. I felt regret that we might never know if they reached Santiago, but in my mind's eye I could see them walking steadily onward just a day ahead of us, inspiring us to continue.

Wolfgang and his wife gave us a warm breakfast and a big hug, sending us off at first light. We soon found a wonderful *panadería,* or bakery, with our noses just as it was opening. We bought fresh, hot bread and silky yogurt for our lunch. The smell almost drove us crazy. I had a desperate time refraining from eating everything right on the spot! We passed through modern Pamplona and on to the gorgeously manicured campus of the university. It could have doubled as a botanical garden with its diverse displays of trees, varied shrubs, sweeping lawns, and flowers just beginning to blossom.

Leaving the city, we continued up a long hill to the tiny town of Cizur Menor. The twelfth century Romanesque church of San Miguel the Archangel, shining in the morning sun, topped the village. We tried to enter and see the inside, but like most of the other churches along the way, it was locked. I could not understand why the churches were invariably closed tight, especially along the Camino. The Camino continues to be one of the major pilgrimage routes in all of Christendom. After all, many of us came to see the art and architecture within the churches, as well as immerse ourselves in the spiritual environment, along the Way of St. James. *Why is it that the churches were all closed and the bars were all open?* The church bell tower is usually the highest point in town, and also marks the center of activity, so one naturally heads right for it like a beacon. Additionally, the yellow arrows and scallop shell symbols directed us every step of the way along the Camino and invariably led to the churches at the heart of every village and city. We were rapidly becoming trained to follow them wherever they led us without question. The Mother Church is really missing a good opportunity here. If they just opened their doors and served coffee, they would have a whole new batch of converts trained to make a beeline for the nearest church as soon as they arrived in town! Seriously, it seems very odd that the Catholic Church is one of the richest entities in the world and it does not place a priority on keeping the lovely, historic churches along the Way of St. James open to pilgrims and citizens alike. What a difference it would make to hire someone from the town to keep the churches open. It would be such a small price for the Catholic Church in Rome to pay, benefiting the citizens of the town and pilgrims alike. Many of us would be willing to make a *donativo* (donation) to help defray the costs. The churches should be a place of refuge to all people. Kept open, they could once again become a place of wonder and mystery as well as one of beauty. They could be a true sanctuary as once intended, a place to sit and rest your body and your mind, seek shelter from the storm, and ask for guidance. Locked tight, they sent an entirely different message.

We traversed beautiful rolling hills that were intensely green with the new spring wheat crop. Up the steep and rocky trail we climbed and climbed until we reached the summit of Alto de Perdón, a twelve-hundred-foot-altitude gain in only a couple of miles. The wind was fierce and constant during the climb. When we reached the top, the wind blew so strongly that we could barely stand up. We had to hold on to our hats and use our trekking poles to lean into the wind or risk being blown back down to the valley far below. Gigantic new windmills that supply clean power to this entire region, as far as the eye could see, topped the entire ridgeline. They sounded like jet engines as we stood beneath them. I stood looking westward on tired legs, suspicious of every hill and mountaintop, wondering how many we would be required to summit. We dropped steeply down the rocky pathway to the next plain. Below us spread miles of undulating wheat fields and huge areas of black plastic reflecting the sun like mirrors. These mysterious plastic farms turned out to be growing white asparagus, a

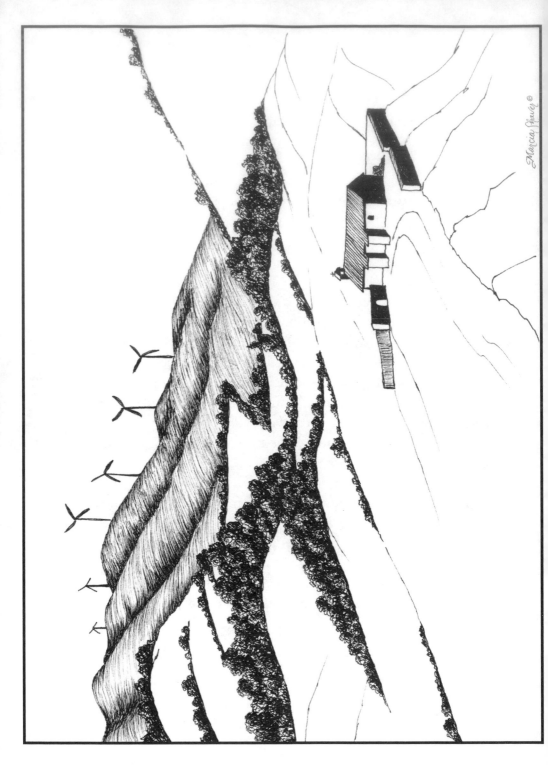

New windmills line many hilltops, in sharp contrast with ancient villages

delicacy of the region. We stopped to eat our picnic of oranges, bread, and lemon yogurt on a dry hillside surrounded by holly and small oak trees, basking in the sunshine.

Soon we made our way to a beautiful little shrine of Mary nestled serenely in a grove of trees. As I sat resting on the long stone bench in Mary's serene presence, it struck me as ironic that as Christians we say there is only one God. Yet we count God the Father God (1), God the Son, or Jesus (2), and God the Holy Ghost or Spirit (3), and have elevated Mary to goddess status as Holy Mary, Mother of God (4). Why be judgmental of the pagans for worshiping multiple gods when it appears we do essentially the same thing? Why condemn idol worshipers when we have statues, crucifixes, and paintings (idols) that we revere and pray in the presence of? Our ideas seem similar to me. Like them, we believe in divine beings greater than ourselves from whom we seek guidance and blessings. Can you imagine how peaceful and productive our world would be if we just let everyone practice their own variation of the same theme? All of the great religions have many of the same basic concepts at the heart of their teachings. Wouldn't God, or the gods, be happy if we could only live this principle? Why do we choose to focus on the differences and the violent teachings? So many of the wars and atrocities throughout history have been perpetrated in the name of religion. The crusades, the Spanish Inquisition, and the current Muslim Jihad against western ideology stand out as particularly brutal examples of this flawed thinking.

We crossed an open windy field to the lovely little town of Uterga and checked into a great, new, privately run albergue. We drew beside the church until the wind tunnel effect drove us back into the café. As we passed the fountain, we found our Danish roommate from last night. She was struggling with massively blistered feet and looked completely worn out but was determined to go on. I offered her a cup of coffee and a rest, so we helped her back to the albergue. I was worried about her health, both mental and physical. By setting unrealistic expectations, she would surely hurt herself, and was setting herself up for a crushing failure. She was determined to finish the Camino in thirty days and lose weight, so she was walking twenty miles per day without stopping and eating only five hundred calories. Not surprisingly, she had no energy and could barely put one foot in front of the other. Despite her very fair skin, she wore no hat, so she was already *very* sunburned. She walked eleven hours the first day from St. Jean Pied de Port to Roncesvalles. And now she said that she was in so much pain that even her skin hurt. This morning she could barely walk from the pain, so I could not believe she had even gotten up and started off, let alone made it this far. She was trying to cover another six or seven miles tonight, even though she did not leave us until after six in the evening. As we tried to talk her into stopping for the day, we heard her story.

She had trained as a professional singer. Several years ago she had a terribly crushing critique from a leading teacher and performer in her country. Not only was the woman cruel and dismissive of her training and ability, she would not tell her what she was doing wrong or how to improve. That one bad teacher humiliated her, and years later her heart still hurt. She lost her confidence, stopped performing, and has been riddled with depression and self-doubt. Worst of all, she turned her back on her gift. She challenged herself to do the Camino to help overcome those issues of inadequacy. But she would never make it to Santiago if she continued like this, and she would be even more disappointed with herself. My heart ached for her. She should have been proud of herself for having done so well, being so very determined, and having such heart in the face of the physical pain. To be so hard on herself is a tragedy. We tried to tell her not to let that one woman turn her from her dream and have such intense power over her. We sent her off with hugs and told her to go out and believe in herself. As she carried her cross into the sunset, a sudden revelation struck me: I am just like her. Because I think I can do it all, I take on too many large projects at one time. I succeed at some and invariably fail at others, making me feel less than who I am. We all need to be gentler with ourselves and bask in the successes we do achieve.

Like that woman, the people you meet on the Camino remind you of what matters most in life:

- Francois who could see nothing made me grateful for everything I could see. Yet even without his sight, he was there walking the same way and getting other benefits from the voyage.

- Martien seemed gentle and quirky and a bit out there in his beliefs, but he accepted everyone. He was very appreciative of being cared about and taken care of and in turn he folded each of us into his caring.

- Our Danish friend reminded me not to be so hard on myself and be proud of what I had accomplished, even if it was not all that I had set out to do. She was an inspiration just to keep trying, keep going on.

- Some of the other pilgrims just rushed on toward their destinations without stopping to look at their surroundings and enjoy what lay before them. They sacrificed the moment for clocking many kilometers each day. That was not how I wished to live my life.

- The sexually enthusiastic and gymnastic German couple who we had met in Viskarret showed up again tonight. Within moments of their arrival, we heard distinct noises and the moving of furniture. We thought, "This can't be," but it continued long enough that we had to just sit there and admire their supernatural energy and zest. That kind of passion for another human being is a thing of beauty.

Uterga to Cirauqui via Eunante
27,649 Steps, 11.78 Miles
April 7

We woke to deep violet, starry skies. As the light crept over the landscape, the sky turned lavender, soft rosy pink, and finally clear cobalt blue in every direction. The morning air was crisp as we wound our way through green hills to Eunante, the site of an octagonal twelfth-century church linked to the Knights Templar. Standing alone in its perfection, it spoke to me of what it must have been like to be a pilgrim hundreds of years ago. It glowed in the early morning light, the golden and reddish colored stones alternating in lovely patterns. The column capitals were carved with palm fronds, faces, and intertwining vines. The supports on the walls featured unique carvings of faces peering down at us, monsters and gargoyles, humans and animals. Some were eroded almost completely away, and others were in quite good condition. We wondered if the direction of the wind or exposure to rain versus being in a more sheltered, covered area that made the difference. Or have some of the carvings been replaced or restored? There is an outer octagonal wall composed of fine double columns and arches mirroring the shape of the main church. A very peaceful, solid, rounded Romanesque church, it seemed to have always been there, emerging naturally from the earth.

As we left Eunante behind us, we came to where some workmen were digging a major ditch with big equipment. It was approximately ten feet deep and several feet wide, composed of slippery wet mud. We had to climb all the way down inside of it in the mud and then crawl out, with our packs on. I doubt that the medieval pilgrims had to face backhoes.

We began to see stork nests everywhere. The huge structures, about six feet across and built with sticks about three feet long and four inches thick, topped church spires, most tall structures, and whatever else most inconvenienced the people who lived here. The storks have been constructing their nests in this fashion on manmade buildings since medieval times. The nests are occupied year after year, and some have been in continuous use for hundreds of years. Both the males and females build or remodel the nests together each year and feed the babies. They are monogamous during the breeding season, then part company for the rest of the year. Usually the storks choose a different mate each year. However, sometimes they pair again the next year, apparently because they particularly like the nest they built. Long bright red-orange legs and beaks contrast sharply with their sleek white bodies and black wings. Before landing in the nests, they circled lazily several times. They were quite graceful in flight and very active. This time of year they had eggs and fledglings to care for. We learned that they feed on the plentiful frogs, insects, tadpoles, and small fish that live in the wetlands of this entire region. We saw them on the ground gathering food, in flight, and feeding their babies all the way from Óbanos to Astorga.

At Puente la Reina we found our first open church, the Iglesia de Santiago. It had fantastic carvings of monsters welcoming the sinners to hell, a sight frightening enough to convince people to be good. Inside a massive gold *retablo*, or large intricate screen, formed the backdrop for the altar, complete with many statues. We wondered if all that gold was plunder from the New World. Had that same gold once been reverently formed by pre-Columbian artists into the gods of the Americas, only to be disrespectfully melted down and shipped to Spain? I could never imagine the conquistadors confessing their mistreatment of the natives. But if they had, what would their priests have said? Would they have ordered them to return all that precious gold? No way. I could hear them saying, "You have preyed on the beliefs of another society by claiming to be the reincarnation of their god. You ruthlessly took their lands and their gold, decimated their population with disease, and destroyed their civilization. I know they are savages who offer human sacrifices to their gods, so we will make them see the error of their ways. Just wait until they see what we have to offer them with the Inquisition! Perhaps you should repent and give all of the riches to the church and queen before you go back to do it again." It does not make sense to justify such ruthless actions all in the name of a supreme being. The Church and the monarchy perverted their power through the conquistadors under their banner. How can we live with ourselves if we treat fellow human beings in such a way, all in the name of a specific religion? We are wrong, and we need to go back to the basic teaching, "Treat others as you would like to be treated."

After visiting the church, we continued across the magnificent six-arched Romanesque bridge spanning the now wide, slow moving Río Arga. The Queen's Bridge, or Puente la Reina, was built in the eleventh century specifically so that pilgrims could cross the river without paying exorbitant prices to men operating the ferries. The creamy yellow stone, pointed arches, and stair-step pilings descended to meet the water's surface, reflecting spectacularly in the quiet green mirror of the river.

The weather began to change just out of Puente la Reina. A cold wind came up, accompanied by dark, sinister clouds. We passed many beautiful farms and "plastic crops," lanes filled with flowering trees and fragrant wildflowers. They smelled so good that we had to take a closer sniff, and Tannis came up with pollen on her nose. We made a hard climb, and when we reached the small village of Mañeru, I was so tired that I wanted to stop. All of a sudden, I felt as if someone had just pulled the plug and drained all of my energy away. I was very footsore. But it did not feel right to stop, so we pushed on through the town, and around the very first bend we were rewarded with a storybook scene. Ahead loomed our destination, Cirauqui. It was a whitewashed town, spilling down from a hilltop to form a crown on the green, undulating farmland. The pathway leading to the town seemed like the yellow brick road as it wound through vineyards and olive groves to a magical destination. Once inside the city walls, the narrow streets twisted steeply up to the center of the town. I derived so much satisfaction from reaching our albergue across from the church, and I reflected on how I had almost not made it. I think that sometimes we make a huge effort and then quit just before reaching our goal. It felt so good to see our destination just moments after feeling like giving up. It recharged us and gave us the extra energy to make that last hill to victory.

The weather had turned suddenly cold, and I got very chilled. After a shower, I got into my sleeping bag with an extra blanket, a silk sheet,

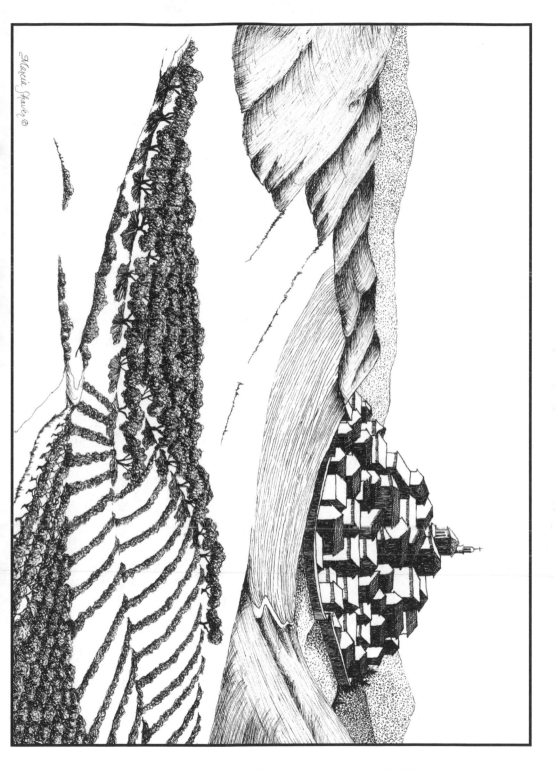

The 9th century hilltop village of Cirauqui, surrounded by vineyards and olive groves

and all of my clothes on. I was still shivering, but a hot cup of tea and a nap worked wonders. We recovered and explored this beautiful town before attending the pilgrim's mass in the thirteenth-century church.

Our dinner was served in the old stone, barrel-vaulted wine cellar of our albergue. What a fantastic room it was, full of medieval atmosphere. Our host's husband cooked us a delicious dinner of soup, pasta, meatballs, yogurt, and fresh fruit, including juicy strawberries from the south of Spain. The local red wine was served in handmade, brightly painted terra cotta pitchers. Fantastically, we were now walking through the famed Rioja region, offering over a thousand different local wines. The vines were first introduced in Roman times and have been continuously cultivated. In AD 950, the region's vineyards expanded significantly due to the Camino de Santiago! The Camino traverses the entire length of the Rioja region, and the increased pilgrim traffic expanded the demand for wine. In the 1850s, a destructive mildew badly damaged the vineyards of Bordeaux, which brought the French to this region with their winemaking techniques. This long history of beautiful grapes and artful winemaking combined to give us a varied, exquisite red wine experience. We had a tasty new surprise for our mouths every night at dinner. The best part was that the wine was included in your pilgrim's meal at the same price as bottled water. I mean come on now, what would you choose? I don't think the Spanish even consider wine to be alcohol because it is so prevalent.

There was great camaraderie of the assembled guests representing the countries of Hungary, Ireland, Poland, France, Canada, and America. Laughter and good food seem to be a universal language, bridging the gaps in language skills. It was so fantastic to meet people from everywhere, sharing dinner, and being kind to one another, all walking to Santiago. We need to find a way to make our world like this. I know there is always a bully and the stakes are very high in a nuclear world, but we can do better if we would just try to walk on together.

Cirauqui to Estella
25,160 Steps, 10.72 Miles
April 8

It started to rain in the night, and everything felt clean and fresh by morning. We donned our full rain gear and set out in drizzle as we regretfully wound our way out of Cirauqui. We crossed a Roman bridge over a deep gorge and walked on the original Roman road for several miles, interspersed with gravel sections. It is some of the best preserved Roman road on the Camino and is amazing that it is still here at all. We crossed many hills lined with vineyards following the contours of the land in lovely patterns. The grapes were starting to send out tender shoots, and everywhere we saw wild rosemary bushes, red poppies, purple irises, tulips, flowering shrubs, and an abundance of yellow flowers, side by side with cactus.

The rain stopped after about an hour, and we peeled off our rain gear. It got very warm and pleasant with dramatic clouds gathering on the horizon. The way was very muddy, and our boots weighed about five pounds each with the accumulating slippery red goo. It made the miles seem longer and our legs more tired.

After passing a modern aqueduct, we crossed a small river on a medieval bridge. It was hard to believe that that perfect bridge has been here for a thousand years and the Roman Road a thousand years before that. We understood that the stream was brackish or poisonous in the Middle Ages. People and horses that drank from it died. They were immediately set upon by unsavory types who lurked nearby to take advantage of their misfortune and steal their property. I was so thankful for the clean water in my pack. It is just one more reminder of how lucky we are to live today. However, today we also passed a monument to the memory of a Canadian *pirigrina* who died on the Camino in 2002, a *tragicamente*. We had passed many such monuments to modern-day pilgrims who did not make it all the way to Santiago. It is a sobering thought.

In the charming town of Villatuerta, we stopped for café con leche and met Vincent, a young Irish man. He had been walking to Santiago and decided to stay and work as a volunteer at the albergue. As an artist without a time constraints, he had the freedom to stay and enjoy the Camino to its fullest. He was also perfecting his Spanish, drawing, and planning to stay until he was "ready to move on." It is wonderful that one can volunteer anywhere along the Camino for food and a room for a time period ranging from a week to a year in each location. He also told us about WWOOF (World Wide Opportunities on Organic Farms), an organization which enables people to work in exchange for room, board, and the opportunity to learn organic farming techniques. Wouldn't it be great to be young and free of responsibility, traveling to wherever the notion takes you?

After traveling through lovely olive groves, we came into Estella. We were greeted by an extremely scary twelfth-century Gothic church façade, featuring fantastic sculptures of all kinds of creatures. Winged monkey demons and all sorts of monsters eating the sinners and stuffing them into the mouth of Hell populated one side. A black coating—from mold or pollution—covered the scenes and added to the sinister look. It was the most amazing thing I have ever seen and powerfully transported us back to a time when the powers of the Church enforced proper behavior through fear and superstition. This was an example of the "scare the hell out of you" philosophy at its finest.

The town of Estella, meaning "star" in Spanish, is set at the base of dramatic cliffs. Snuggled close to the cliff wall sits the massive Church of San Pedro de la Rúa, where the kings of Navarre once swore their oaths. It was severely damaged in 1572 when one of the local rulers blew up the castle above it. The castle foundations can still be seen clinging to the high ground and marked by a cross.

We sat on a bench and drew for several hours in the warm sunshine. Hilariously enough, large trucks intermittently parked *right in front of us*, totally blocking our view. After ten days on the Camino, we just smiled and worked on a different part of our drawings until they departed. We rewarded our good behavior by purchasing ten euros' worth of the most decadent chocolate I had ever tasted. I am

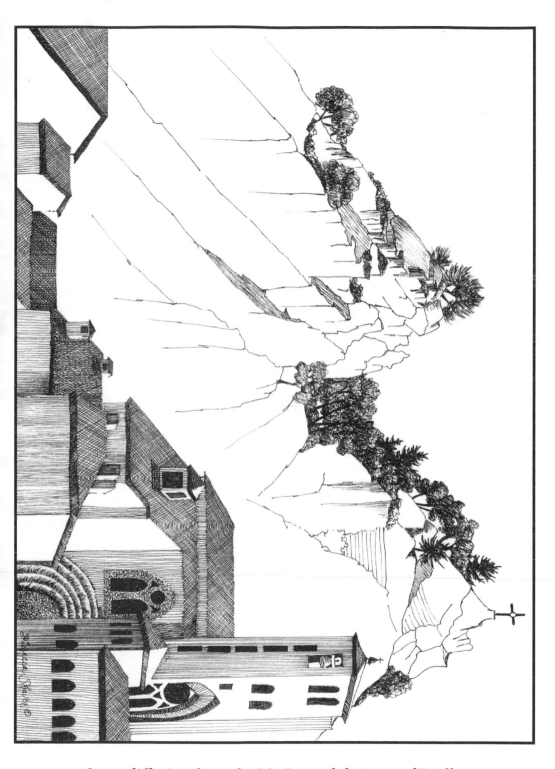

Steep cliffs rise above the Río Ega and the town of Estella

surprised that this chocolate was not portrayed on the Heaven side of that church portal. Piously, we decided that we needed it to keep up our strength on the road. We bought bread and cheese to salve our conscience, but that heavenly white chocolate was truly to die for, a perfect end to a good day.

Estella to Los Arcos
31,412 Steps, 13.38 Miles
April 9

I was eating the giant croutons/ toast for breakfast and in walked Martien with his headlight on! He practically blinded me. I thought he had risen before dawn and had just walked in from some other village in the dark. It turned out that he had slept upstairs in the hallway. I guess he just had to use the guy gadget headlight thing. We were so happy to see him again.

We set out of Estella and soon came to a great Spanish tradition, a *fuente del vino*—a fountain from the local wine producers that flows with awesome red wine, all you can drink. It had a sign telling you not to overindulge, but I mean, *come on*! Get serious. It was extremely tasty, but we arrived unprepared and had no container to fill for our voyage. We had to make do with a few sips straight out of the faucet using our cupped hands.

Right beside the road stood the massive Monasterio de Irache that had been in existence since the tenth century and only closed in the 1980s due to lack of new monks joining the brotherhood. The adjoining hospital was founded in 1050 to take care of sick pilgrims. (Possibly also caring for those who might have overindulged at the fuente del vino and decided they were finished walking for the day?) Thinking of something lasting so many centuries overwhelmed me. In America, we call a two-hundred-year-old building old, but that pales besides these ancient structures.

We had very muddy trails today. We skirted beautiful Montejurra Mountain, covered with pine and oak forests and interspersed

Monjardín's peak is crowned by Castillo San Esteban

with the occasional olive tree. We heard the song of cuckoo birds for the first time. The wildflowers set off the spectacular views across the valleys below us. In the distance loomed a tall mountain with a fairy-tale castle and church on top. This was Monjardín, which has been a strategic military site throughout time. The castle had Roman origins but is best known as one of the last strongholds of the Islamic Moors in the Christian re-conquest of Spain. They fought a great battle in these valleys and mountains against the Spanish and, some say, the French.

We emerged from the forests to the tiny town of Luquín. It was filled with lovingly cared for, clean houses, most featuring very impressive coats of arms on the walls. We crossed miles of rolling green farmland and met a German man named Helmut. Is that a classic German name or what? He was about seventy, very robust and jolly, sporting a green felt German hat and carrying a hand-carved walking staff. He had carved the stick himself over the winter, embellishing it with symbols person-ally meaningful, in thoughtful preparation for his journey. We walked together and chatted until he "stopped to make rest." Meeting Helmut typified the way we walked with others along the Camino. Tannis and I ambled along at our own pace much of the time without the company of others. When we encountered new people, we greeted each other and continued on together for a time in a comfortable camaraderie. Everyone kept his or her own pace and the distances covered each day varied. We might say goodbye to someone, only to meet him or her again days or weeks later. Although it seemed as if we were walking alone much of the time, if we sat down, not more than thirty minutes would pass before another pilgrim crossed our path. The meeting and parting created a rhythmic ebb and flow, providing both continuity with others and solitude for us along the way.

My toes felt as if they had been squeezed in a vice, and the bot-toms of my feet felt as if some evil creature had been hitting them with a hammer. They are very bruised from the extra weight of the pack for so many miles each day. When we arrived today and took showers, I noticed that the toenails were all squishy and loose. They were begin-ning to turn purple, and a doctor staying here informed me that I will lose them. However, the purple toenails and bruised foot pads form a nice color harmony in violet.

Tonight we went out into the plaza and there sat Martien, along with Helmut. We told them we would be right back because we were going to check out the church. It was obviously open, a rare thing, as music and singing were escaping from it and floating out into the plaza. We found a packed house with standing room only—with good reason. What a wonderful experience. We got to hear the pipe organ blended with the voices of the congregation filling the entire church. All the while, we got a great look at the Gothic cloister and the heavy gold Baroque interior. I wondered about a wooden panel painting that looked Renaissance, but I refrained from walking over to examine it because we were obviously attending a mass. We could not follow the prayers in Spanish, but we bowed our heads and mumbled. We were sort of wedged between the holy water fountain and the columns at the back of the church. After a final song, the priest walked around the front of the church, chanting, while carrying with a big, ornate silver cross that also looked a bit like a reliquary. I was just thinking how lucky we were to be part of some local celebration when the silver cross rounded the corner followed by a casket. I *could not believe* we had crashed a funeral! How embarrassing can you get? At least we were respectful, but *JEEZ!* I guess they can't exactly post a "No Tourists" sign whenever they want to use their own church.

We emerged to find Martien and Helmut still at the table with a bottle of wine for us. Maude, a sixty-nine-year-old German woman, had joined them. We all shared dinner and heard Maude's story. She had breast cancer and went through the surgery and now was walking the Camino with a group of twelve other women who had breast cancer. They were participating in a study with a German university to see if exercise, fresh air, no stress, and being outside all day have an effect on the healing process and re-occurrence rate for cancer patients. Later we met and walked with two other amazing women who were part of the study. The same university had conducted an earlier study where a group of women had stayed in very cold temperatures, lived outside all day, and slept in igloos. This was a follow-up study. What an amazing concept for a university to study these factors as part of the healing process. I wondered if they figured in the variable of prayer. That would be *really* interesting, but I do not know how they would separate it from the rest of the experience. I believe stress plays a big role in causing cancers. White haired Maude certainly did not show any signs of stress. Robust, smiling, and energetic, despite her age, she was keeping up with our pace. What an inspiration!

Los Arcos to Viana
34,554 Steps, 14.72 Miles
April 10

My earplugs are fantastic! I was the last one awake after a much-needed rest. The albergue hosts let me sleep longer after Tannis told them what a hard time I had yesterday. Eventually I was awakened by the melodies of Bob Marley floating through the air.

We met the youngest pilgrim of our journey this morning. He was five years old, walking the Camino with his mother. They walk about five miles a day, and he seems able to do that much distance cheerfully. He is an adorable little blond German pilgrim, dressed in miniature khaki pants with zip-off legs. Whooping like a cowboy, he was riding around the albergue on his toy plastic dinosaur. The night before, he had slept with a tiny teddy bear, which was tied to the back of his mother's pack as they set off. How will this journey influence his future? My son says he cannot remember any specific events before approximately six years of age, but he knows he was happy and secure.

We put on our rain gear and headed out. We exited through the magnificently carved city gates and appropriately past the cemetery with the freshly interred fellow from last night's funeral. We paused to say a prayer and apologize for our intrusion last night.

The countryside opened up into rolling hills ringed by beautiful rugged mountains, and we noticed fewer farm animals and more vine-yards in this region. The red earth is so dark and fertile that in places it appears to be almost purple. The rain had turned the trails into red glue, and every step was a sucking process with boots that continually gained pounds. It made for slippery going, and our legs were feeling the additional resistance. We suspected that the miles between points on the way must be measured via the road or as the crow flies rather based on the actual distance walked. What began as a short day seemed very long by the time we arrived in Viana. The skies were a dramatic deep blue gray and deluged us with a ferocious downpour for a couple of hours. We passed many round, ancient-looking little stone huts. As the storm continued, we began to wonder if our trekking poles would act like lightning rods and considered taking shelter in one of them when lightning began striking very close to us. Just then the sun came out, and for the rest of the day it rained only intermittently. Despite the rain, the countryside was so very beautiful. Of course, coming from Seattle, we rarely considered such weather terrible. Anyone who does simply has inappropriate clothing or the wrong attitude.

As our route paralleled the highway, a huge bike race surrounded us. The brightly colored team jerseys, support cars, and blaring music added a different excitement to our journey. It was a five-day bike race, somewhat like a tour de España, and seemed to be a very big competition here in Spain. After the quiet of the Camino, it was ridiculously exciting. We waved at the TV cameras speeding by and cheered the riders.

We came to Torres del Río, twin towns facing each other with a river and gorge separating them. They were walled medieval towns topped by church spires, looking very magical in the sunshine and glistening with the recent rain. We visited the church Iglesia de Santo Sepulcro, built in the 1100s. It featured a vaulted ceiling with crisscrossed arches, and the rib vaulting formed an eight-sided star. Lace stone window screens, which looked Arabic, and other features showed the influence of various cultures in its blended architecture. Most unusual was its round dome rising above an octagonal floor. As we looked up into the dome, we saw a decorative checkerboard motif all the way around. It is thought to be linked to the Knights Templar and the church of the Holy Sepulchre in Jerusalem. The design struck me as both complex and simple at the same time, very beautiful and serene.

Outside again, we slogged on through the mud to loud thunder as we approached the outskirts of Viana. We both could barely lift our boots one more step. When we consulted our books, we were dismayed to discover the albergue was on the far side of this steep town. I lay on a nearby picnic table with my pack still on my back and my boots (now weighing twenty pounds each) hanging off the end. Wahhh! I whined pathetically, but since we had nobody to beam us over to our destination, we just got up and walked onward.

We found our very nice Albergue Andres Munoz. Right next to it was the ruin of a fantastic Gothic church, the Iglesia de San Pedro, dating to the early thirteenth century. It collapsed in the 1830s, and the vaults remain open to the sky. The huge broken shapes made a very dramatic, graphically stark silhouette against the heavens. Inside the albergue, the bunks were three high and looked flimsy. I was on the bottom, Tannis was in the middle, and we fervently hoped that we would not be under a five-hundred-pound German. "News Flash! American pilgrims on the way to the holy city of Santiago crushed in the their sleep by German panzer!" We took a much-needed shower, and I washed off so much mud that I clogged up the plumbing. Seriously, I created a mudflow that would have made Mt. St. Helens proud. I was so dirty and wet and tired it was unbelievable. Rejuvenated post shower, we limped off to café con leche and pastries in the square, shadowed by the gigantic Iglesia de Santa Maria church. It had ornately decorated carvings in high relief and very lifelike figures, as they were carved in the Renaissance instead of Gothic times. We sat out in the Plaza de los Fueros with the five o'clock sunshine blazing and illuminating the fountain, the church façade, and the ornate building across the way, which was flying brightly colored flags. I began to draw, and five minutes later, it began to rain. How did that happen? The city streets were so narrow that you seemed to be in a warren. We apparently had begun to draw in the one patch of blue sky for miles around; we just did not know it.

The streets of Viana were filled with stunning family crests and flower-filled ironwork balconies. Intricate iron gates graced the streets. The walls of this hilltop city have Roman origins, and the city itself was

The 13th century walled city of Viana is graced with handsome, carved family crests and flower filled balconies.

founded in 1219. It withstood many sieges over the centuries and was an important pilgrimage stop. Now it was undergoing much urban renewal. But, instead of sprawling out into suburbia, the people were staying in these tiny towns and keeping the old intact. Owners of the centuries-old houses were demolishing only the insides, retaining the façades to blend with the rest of the town. This kept the small towns neat and alive instead of abandoned and shabby.

We were so famished by seven thirty that we went to the hotel bar in search of food. "*No, OCHO MEDIA.*" Eight thirty! Fearing we would perish in an hour, we ordered a bottle of wine and sat salivating like Pavlov's dogs until the eight-thirty dinner service. I could not understand! I was in a restaurant. Restaurants serve food. I was hungry and had money. But it would not feed me until eight thirty, no matter what, not so much as a peanut. It is a quirk of Spanish culture one must simply accept because finding an alternative is futile.

Tonight before dinner, we heard Martien's story of grief and loss. As a young man he had been married and divorced, but he and his former wife shared a beautiful four-year-old son. He was seeing another woman, and they had taken the boy on a vacation together. The child drowned accidentally, and Martien was devastated. What parents have not lost sight of their child for a few moments in a busy place? To his horror, the grandmother accused Martien of killing the child and then tossing him in the water to give the appearance of an accident. She thought he wanted a responsibility-free life with the new woman. An autopsy was performed on the child to determine if there was water in his lungs, indicating a drowning, or just air, indicating he had been killed first. During the course of his story, Martien's voice became quieter and more halting. Looking into the distance, as if the scene was still before him, he said quietly, "When I first saw him he looked like a sleeping angel. After the operation his little body was all bruised and cut up. It was horrible." I have never seen a man's face just crumple in despair like that. He began to sob uncontrollably. As his body shook, we hugged him and held his hand. By hearing him with an open heart, we hoped we were helping him release the grief, which he had carried with him for so very long. What a terrible image of his child that must have been to hold in his heart for all those years. He had kept his story inside, never telling anyone. I hoped that our complete acceptance of him without judgment would be a turning point, allowing his healing process to begin. He was a gentle soul and must have suffered beyond imagination carrying that burden.

I thought about Martien sharing his sorrow with us, relative strangers. He would never have to see Tannis and me again if he so chose. Did he select us because he hardly knew us? Do people find it easier to give our secrets to a stranger than someone we see every day? I felt deeply honored that Martien had entrusted me with the story so close to his heart.

Viana to Logroño
17,545 Steps, 7.5 Miles
April 11

The oompah-pah of snoring caused a restless night for Tannis, and the situation escalated when people created an atomic level disturbance rustling plastic bags and packs at 6 in the morning. Shortly after, they threw the lights on and began seriously making noise while trapping Tannis in her middle bunk because they had monopolized all the floor space. Craftily, I had slipped out in the dark at 5:45 to go downstairs and catch up on my journal entries.

An icy wind was blowing, and new snow lay very low on the surrounding mountains. The thought of venturing out in such weather did not sit well with us, more so because of our physical condition than the outside conditions. Tired and footsore, Tannis and I both had saddle sores. I had a rub under my arm, and her hipbones were raw. Fortunately, I had enough padding there that that would never happen to me. Even her poor belly button was raw, which was most bizarre. My toenails had turned purple and threatened to fall off any day. We decided we needed a rest day so we walked the very short seven and a half miles to Logroño and found a nice little hotel. We pampered ourselves with the luxuries of a bathtub, heat, and only the two of us sleeping in the

Near the town of Logroño, in the heart of the Rioja wine region

room. We went out and proceeded to eat and drink ourselves into a stupor and then slept the entire afternoon away. The "Chanel Pilgrim" had had enough!

The elegant town of Logroño bustled with activity, and we soaked up its history. One church had ornate twin towers and an impressive Gothic interior. We visited another older church, built around 1000 but sitting on top of one built in the 800s. The center of town featured an arched, covered walkway lined with very sophisticated, upscale shops and restaurants. I felt like a hick in my pilgrim's attire, but as usual, the gracious Spanish never made us feel out of place. Even the parks reflected the town's elegance with their big fountains and beautiful flowers. We had chosen a good day—and place—to rest, but we wondered if we would be able to start again tomorrow.

On our walk into Logroño that morning, we had come to a tiny house where the señora had invited us in for café and cookies. Her name was Maria. She and her mother before her, Felicia, have welcomed pilgrims for years. In kindness, she had moved the heater near me when she saw that I was shivering. Her house was tiny, a one-room kitchen and living area with a wood-burning stove. Chopped wood had sat neatly stacked under a staircase that led, presumably, to her bedroom. Dried tomatoes and corn had hung from the stairs, and she had kept her few cooking utensils arranged on the white wall. Outside she had had pots of flowers and her little dog, who did tricks. She had had so little, and yet she had offered her hospitality so freely. But, really, she had had all one needed, and I felt that I could live like that. She had not apologized for her simple home, but instead she had just offered shelter, a hot drink, and a smile.

Here on the Camino, we had found a sanctuary, which had awakened in us a sense of how little we really need. It had reminded us that "need" and "want" are vastly different. For the first time, many of us realize that a warm, dry place to sleep, the luxury of having enough to eat, a change of clothes, a bar of soap, and a good companion to share the miles with completely satisfy a person's needs. But most important are the love, the laughter, the learning, and the courage to go on in this journey we call life.

The Camino is a great equalizer. Here we have no fancy cars or houses, no impressive job titles, no designer clothes. Political, cultural, and geographic barriers are minimized. All of the trappings of the outside world, which define many people's image of themselves, vanish. Without those external crutches, we see each other—and ourselves—only in terms of our willingness to help another person, our sense of humor, our kindness, our ability to forgive, listen, share, and accept each other. We learn to rely on ourselves and at the same time have genuine gratitude for what we have received from others. On the Camino, we know for a certainty that we all are literally and figuratively walking down the same road, one that opens onto the pathway to a better world. We simply must find a way to carry this knowledge with us into our everyday lives and change our world.

Logroño to Ventosa
30,385 Steps, 13 Miles
April 12

As we left Logroño with Martien, a very well-dressed Spanish man came up to him waving forty euros and talking in Spanish. Suspiciously, Martien told him no, remembering the time he was in Egypt and a man asked him how many camels he wanted to sell his wife. Not wanting to sell us too cheaply, he rebuffed the man, only to realize many kilometers too late that the forty euros had fallen out of his pocket. The man was just trying to return it. To quote Martien, "SHIST!"

Soon after the euro incident, a man stopped his car and told us we were going the wrong way. It is a good feeling on the Camino that people will help you if you will let them. People look after you, honk and wave to encourage you to go forward. Nearly everyone smiles and enthusiastically greets you with "*Hola! Buenas dias! Buen Camino!*" (Hello! Good day! Have a good walk to Santiago!) That triple greeting in place of just a nod became a sweet rhythm of the Camino. I think everyone is too suspicious of each other in "the real world." We are afraid so we project our fears onto others, and they in turn become afraid and suspicious of us. It seems that if we would always respect others and expect the best of everyone, we might get burned once in a while, but most of the time we would have much more positive interactions.

Steadily we climbed on a wide paved path through miles of vineyards to a lake with pine trees and people fishing. We had a beautiful morning for walking. A bright blue sky set off the opening blossoms of the apple and hazelnut trees, and their subtle scents softly drifted in the air. We reached the small town of Navarrete and stuffed ourselves with fresh, hot ham and eggs in a *bocadilla* amounting to an omelet in an entire loaf of bread. The sidewalk café was packed with young pilgrims eating and laughing in the sunshine. As we were leaving town, we saw an old man in a worn suit, with a silver trumpet and a goat. He played the trumpet, and the goat climbed a ladder and rotated slowly, then lifted its hoof in a salute. He danced for us! It was so hilarious that we laughed until we had tears running down our faces. The goat was soft brown, black, and white colored with golden eyes and a sweet temperament. He allowed us to pet him and left us smiling. We named him Manolo the Dancing Goat of Navarrete. We each gave his owner a euro for entertaining us so well. Some might think that was a mercenary ploy to get money, but so what? I cannot think of a better way to make a living than to make people happy.

We reached the little hilltop town of Ventosa where we stayed. There was an icy wind blowing off the mountains, which are freshly dusted with snow. Although it was a lovely sunny day, it was too windy and cold to draw in the open so we went to the sheltered courtyard of the albergue. It was painted a bright warm yellow and was full of fellow pilgrims. I drew a hand-painted vase on the wall that had petunias casting a long, dramatic diagonal shadow. I decided we should have a party so I bought a couple of bottles of wine, olives, and crackers for only five or six euros. Soon salami, ham, more wine, bread, and more olives appeared. We had a great international impromptu party all afternoon, where I made a miraculous discovery. A girl from Finland, Terttu, also refused to give up her perfume! We had both been under intense pressure but were holding fast. We smugly compared scents and declared in a show of solidarity, "*No huele mal; huele bien!*" which means "We

Manolo the dancing goat

don't smell bad; we smell good!" Her two Canadian friends, Marjorie and Elaine, could not believe there were two perfumed pilgrims with color-coordinated packs, accessories, jackets, and T-shirts inhabiting the same stretch of the Camino.

Terttu looked like an elf with her short, auburn hair in a spiky cut. Her eyes glowed with mischief, and she had such skill in merriment that she confidently made jokes in English. What an admirable talent to understand a second language so well that you grasp the subtleties of humor. Seventy-four-year-old Marjorie had the tall, slender physique of a natural athlete. Her caustic wit and zest for life were contagious. Elaine, short and dark like I was, clearly enjoyed herself to the fullest. She sported a wide smile and the attitude that she just might try anything. The three of them were very funny and made us laugh, smiling all afternoon. After multiple bottles of wine, Martien declared gallantly that he would not part with us for even four thousand euros or an entire herd of camels.

Ventosa to Azofra
25,784 Steps, 11 Miles
April 13

I woke early to cook, as I had purchased breakfast eggs and bread for Tannis, Martien, and me. I sliced the bread, left for a minute, and when I returned half of it was gone. Then a girl asked if it was communal bread, and I said, "No, it is mine, but you can have some." She took half of what was left. That brought my fancy breakfast down to four eggs and three pieces of bread for three hungry travelers! The good news was that I watched the girl pan-fry the bread in olive oil and spices, so I learned a delicious new way to prepare it for the future. The bread incident is also a commentary on how freely things were shared here. I was sure that whoever took the first half of the loaf innocently assumed it had been left for us by the albergue, as sometimes happens.

We laced up and were walking by eight o'clock under clear blue skies, with incredibly beautiful light and dramatic shadows moving

Long shadows fall across the sunny courtyard wall in Ventosa

across the landscape. We were now traversing drier countryside, which was still hilly but less mountainous. Miles of vineyards stretched before us, glowing in the early morning light, which set fire to the red, deeply plowed earth. In contrast, snow again had dusted the mountains all around us, and a sharp crispness hung in the air. We reached the summit of the Alto San Anton surrounded by pine forests and hundreds of stacked pilgrim stones, forming little marker piles. Seeing how many others had gone before us served as sweet encouragement to continue onward. Right after cresting the peak and descending into the next valley, we heard the bleating of many voices. Our investigation revealed a flock of sheep and almost as many lambs—so newly born that they still had their umbilical cords attached. We spent about thirty minutes just watching them play, nurse, and butt each other. They tottered around and climbed on things, already exploring their brand new world. Unbelievably sweet and innocent, their coats matched their nature—soft and whispy. Tannis complimented the mothers, saying, "Strong work ladies!"

As we descended toward Nájera, we came to a stone beehive-shaped structure. Apparently this was an old watchtower and the site of a legendary battle. The Muslim giant Ferragut, descended from Goliath, lived near Nájera and held its Christian citizens captive. All attempts to oust him had failed, and even Charlemagne's troops had been unsuccessful. Eventually, Ferragut and Charlemagne's knight, Roland, fought it out here to the death. Roland prevailed and freed the town of the dreaded Ferragut. It is said that Ferragut had a nose the span of a man's hand and the strength of forty men. That had to be one big, ugly giant! But the hill was lovely with a plain stretching out to the foothills of the distant mountains.

We entered a very poor, run-down, and industrial part of Nájera. That was the first time we had seen such a town in the beautiful and prosperous country of Spain. We stopped for café in a smoky bar filled completely with men. The place offered no food, and the people did not look pleased to see us invading their all-male sanctuary. We departed and walked about a hundred yards further where we came to a lovely bridge crossing a swift river, shining brilliantly in the sun. There were people fishing and strolling in the large park that lined the waterfront. Pink and red cliffs formed a backdrop to the river, with the old town nestled at their feet. You guessed it; the river park was lined with snazzy cafés serving mouthwatering food! We soon were joined by Marjorie, Elaine, and Terttu for Sunday lunch and relaxation. What a different opinion of Nájera we formed in just a hundred yards.

We passed through the clean and well-preserved old quarter of the town. There were very old (1004) monasteries of Santa Maria Real and churches cut into the pink stone. They began as natural caves, where in 1004 a statue of Mary was discovered and a miracle declared. The same reddish pink stone of the cliffs carries forward to form the emerging structures. They are finished off with lovely towered façades and roofs. There was once a jeweled crown here that was stolen in the 1300s and the jewels divided up by Pedro the Cruel. One particularly nice stone was given to Prince Edward, and is known as the Black Prince Ruby. It now shines from the front of the British Coronation Crown.

We climbed up over another small mountain and arrived at the small town of Azofra just as the wind started to howl and the rain began to pour. We opted for a still life drawing of two bottles containing the most excellent Rioja wine of the region. The wine has been fantastically tasty, varied, plentiful, ridiculously inexpensive, and a lubricant for international social contact. It was another Camino miracle. The miles of vines rising up from the red earth continued to lead us through the undulating countryside in a timeless rhythm. The bottles from each winery were unique and lovely, right down to their intricately patterned corks. Drawing the wine was a good choice, as a massive thunder and lightning storm ensued outside, and the wind savagely lashed the rain against the windows. As we drew, our laundry tumbled in the dryer, and we visited with Marjorie, Elaine, and Terttu. The French women provided an impromptu concert with their beautiful voices, singing like angels! The wine, the fine company, the music, and the snacks provided good therapy for my swollen sausage feet with blistered toes and raw, bleeding ankles.

That night at the pilgrims' dinner, we met the highly amusing Bergit and the young Swiss friend she was walking with, Thomas. In

The excellent and varied Rioja wines

order to find something in common with Thomas, we talked about cows, agriculture, and the mountainous country of Switzerland where some of my ancestors came from. We discussed how hard and time consuming it was to milk a cow by hand, compared to the new methods with milking machines. Then Bergit began to tell us the only bad story we were to hear about the Camino. A man had kept looking at her in her bunk in a provocative and lecherous way. She said haltingly, "That vas very uncomfortable because he vas … vell, he vas, um, you know, he ah …" Clearly she was at a loss for words. Being the helpful individual that I am, I asked, "Was he milking the cow?" Thomas immediately turned red, spurted wine out of his nose, and choked on his dinner. Meanwhile, Bergit leapt at the opportunity and triumphantly declared, "Yes! He vas! That is exactly vhat he vas doing, milking his cow!" Thomas had to leave the table. The rest of us remained glued to her story, fascinated by the details, but then we were all women. Marjorie wondered why Bergit had all the luck. After the hilarity calmed down, we told her that she should have reported it because that sort of thing is rare and not tolerated on the Camino. Poor Thomas did not show his face again until dessert. Now it will probably spread around the world that "milking the cow" is American slang for, well, you know!

Azofra to Santo Domingo
27,324 Steps, 11.64 Miles
April 14

An arctic wind was blowing off the frozen mountains, forcing me to wear everything I owned, including my ski hat and gloves, with my Buff over my face like a *bandita*. Still, my ears ached because the wind was so biting and bitterly cold. We climbed steadily across rolling hills of more green wheat fields until we reached, shockingly, a new golf course and condominium development at the crest. I could not imagine what they were thinking, putting a golf course on top of such an exposed hill. Windmills would have made more sense.

Yesterday we met an American woman named Jacqueline, and Martien seemed taken with her. They walked together yesterday and were gone from the albergue this morning. We have been thrown over for another woman! When we stopped for lunch, they were in the bar, so finding them gave us a good opportunity to tell them we were glad they had found each other to walk with because their pace was more suited to one another. Martien was always miles ahead of us, or we were running to keep up because he was so much taller. It felt much better to say good-bye and give him a hug than just having him gone. We once again parted with our friend Martien, wondering if we would ever see him again. I wondered if he needed to separate himself from us because he had confessed something so personal and let us help carry his secret. Regardless, I was so pleased to see his face more relaxed and his spirit lighter and more playful. I prayed that that was in part due to sharing his terrible burden with us two nights ago.

This part of Spain truly felt like home in the American West, with the bonus of a fantasy element. The cultivated fields stretched as far as the eye could see with ribbons of road running through, surrounded on all sides by mountains. Then, just as I began to think I was back home, the vineyards and olive groves climbed the hill and a whitewashed village sat perched at the peak. The combination of the familiar with the unusual gives quite a magical feeling to the area, yet I have also felt so very at home here.

We walked with Elaine today, very much enjoying her company and gentle spirit. She is a genuinely nice person all the way to the core. The miles fell away as we talked of our children, our homes, our husbands, and the challenges of parenthood. We found an easy camaraderie, with laughter interwoven among tales of motherhood and living. This gentle woman then delightfully surprised me when she revealed that she worked as a contractor and built houses. She was tool woman extraordinaire! I was so impressed by the strength, hard work, and organizational skills needed to be a female contractor in a male-dominated profession. I could not help but wonder if men were threatened by a woman with a tool belt. Or did they find it kind of sexy? In these liberated times of strong, independent women, things can get confusing. The old rules no longer apply. How is a woman to know for sure how to accessorize? Let me think a minute, tool belt or garter belt?

We traversed a long broad plateau and then dropped down into Santo Domingo. There lay a fabulous church and a bustling little town. Our albergue was in a beautiful, very old building where you entered a stone interior courtyard after passing through the heavy, iron studded, giant wooden doors. That night, French and German singing groups gave us another spontaneous concert. The old songs, sung so skillfully, filled the building with heartbreakingly lovely melody.

We drew the cathedral, coaxed to stay and driven out of the square by alternating fair weather and cloudbursts with hail flurries of epic proportions. Santo Domingo began construction of the cathedral in the eleventh century, and it is dedicated to him, containing his crypt. The windows are translucent alabaster, framed in high Gothic vaults. We were devastated to learn that the live rooster and hen they **always** kept at the church were not there due to the restoration on the façade! The curious legend says that in the 1300s an innocent young pilgrim was accused of theft and hanged. His parents continued on to Santiago and, upon their return, found him still alive on the gallows. Santo Domingo had intervened to keep him alive because of his innocence. The parents appealed to the magistrate to have their son pardoned and cut down. However, he mocked them with the statement that their son was just as dead as the chickens on his dinner plate. At that point, the chickens stood up and crowed, completing the miracle. The young pilgrim was then pardoned and released to continue home with his parents. A rooster and hen have been kept continuously in the church to celebrate the legend, and it is said that if a pilgrim hears the cockcrow, he or she will have good luck on the journey. Apparently we could not conclude we would have good luck; but then again, the cock's crow had serenaded us along our entire journey. We had already been so fortunate and rich in our experiences that to have expected more would have been greedy.

In keeping with the spirit of Santo Domingo, who spent his life quietly improving the Camino for pilgrims in the eleventh century, we should have been grateful for having seen it at all. Santo Domingo was

Cathedral at Santo Domingo, begun in the 11ᵗʰ century

a study in persistence. Two monasteries rejected him, yet he decided to work for the good of God anyway. He spent his life building his own hermitage on the site of the present-day town, a bridge, a new road, and a hospital. The king rewarded him with the construction of a church in his honor that later became a cathedral. Many miracles have occurred here over the centuries.

Santo Domingo to Grañon, via Yuso and Suso Monasteries
14,327 Steps, 6.1 Miles
April 15

We sadly said good-bye to Marjorie and Elaine. Tannis, Terttu, and I went to visit the nearby World Heritage sites: the monasteries of Yuso and Suso. Getting there went from impossible (tourist office advice) to very complicated (albergue recommendation) to very easy (ask a local). First we were told it was not possible to get there from Santo Domingo. Then we were told we would have to take a bus back to Nájera and then hire a taxi from there. We tried to hire a taxi from here, but not one would even answer the phone. Finally we fell back on our tried and tested plan, eating. At breakfast we approached the señora in the local café, who spoke no English, but helped us out. She fed us a fabulous breakfast while she made some calls. She smilingly told us to leave our packs with her for the day and her friend would take us and later pick us up. What began as impossible yesterday suddenly became a holiday. Soon Jesus arrived to whisk us away to the valley at the foot of the snow-covered mountains we have been walking parallel to. We felt as if we had arrived at Shangri-La because it was so beautiful and so peaceful.

The Monasterio de Yuso sat tucked into a lovely valley with trees flushing-out burnt sienna and lime green surrounded by fields of deep forest green and the snow-capped mountains at its head. With a tall pointed tower, the architecture looked more Swiss in construction. It was very large, with many building phases expanding it over the years.

San Millán Yuso and Suso are two of the oldest monasteries in Europe, linked together as one entity. Monks have continuously occupied them for over fourteen centuries. Fourteen hundred years, can you imagine? This was the birthplace of the Spanish language. In this very spot, an anonymous scholar first wrote down one of the most widely spoken languages in the world. The monastery included a library with exquisitely illuminated books and manuscripts from many different centuries. Several songbooks measured approximately three feet tall and two feet wide. At a time before printing presses allowed for easy and inexpensive duplication of books, the monks, who had sung and chanted from different parts of the church, needed such large versions in order to read them from a great distance. The ancient leather bindings and vibrantly colored illustrated pages, highlighted with gold leaf, took my breath away with their beauty. They looked so fragile, yet they had been in this very place for centuries.

The much older monastery of Suso was built into the cliffs and surrounded by pine trees. Construction began where a crack in the rocks opened to many natural caves. The remains of San Millan still rest there. The whole area vibrated with the quiet intensity of a truly holy place, timeworn and holding the secrets of the ages, and evoked a hush serenity, the core of peace itself. The building was a pinkish stone, and the arches and pillars of great antiquity looked like keyholes into eternity. They echoed various architectural periods and styles—Arabic, Romanesque, Gothic, and Asian—all at one time yet successfully combined them in a single unique motif. It is very magical, a place indefinable and completely unto itself.

Just as we were contemplating lunch, our taxi showed up one hour early in order not to interfere with the driver's nap. Since you do not argue with Jesus when he shows up at a holy place, even if he is in the form of a toothless Spanish taxi driver, we returned to Santo Domingo. Obviously, we had to have a big lunch in the nice señora's restaurante and leave a huge tip expressing our gratitude that she had made it possible for us to have the magical experience at the monasteries.

The monasteries of San Millán Yuso and Suso

And naturally, lunch included a full bottle of the local red wine. This was a lot of fun, but we soon realized the error of our ways when we had to hoist our packs and walk in the heat of the day the six measly miles to Grañon. Any self-respecting Spaniard would have been taking his siesta at that hour, especially after that massive carbohydrate-filled lunch and the wine. We soon pitted out. Panties le Pew. We began to consider desperate measures. Terttu said we could hijack a farmer. Of course she meant hitchhike, but in our state we found alternative interpretations hilarious. "News Flash! Farmer accosted by three wine soaked pilgrims on the Camino de Santiago! Tractor stolen! Entire year's harvest at risk!" Those farmers had reason to watch out because I know how to drive a tractor.

The albergue at Grañon was fantastic, situated in a very romantic medieval bell tower built in the 1200s. The round windows of the church were deep-set, cream-colored stone. Simple yet elegant ironwork imbedded into the stone cast a shadowy replica of itself into the deep recesses. We were taken to the bell tower for a view of the town, climbing its stone steps so worn from thousands of feet treading them that they were scooped out. At the top, the people proudly and excitedly showed us everything in their unique corner of the world.

The communal hall upstairs had long tables, a fireplace, and shuttered windows. Despite the tight quarters—we slept on the floor on gym mats right next to each other, and only three bathrooms served close to sixty people—the aubergue and its people exuded an amazing spirit. We went to the pilgrims' church service, conducted by a charismatic priest in his forties. He glowed with caring, compassion, and welcome. He recognized each of us personally by nationality and gave us a special, sincere blessing in English and Spanish. After the mass, we went upstairs to prepare a communal dinner, consisting of bread, fresh salad, and fantastic lentil soup. The priest in his plaid shirt joined us at the meal, talking to each of us individually. He simply said, "You are always welcome here. Come back and be a volunteer. This will be your home. You will always have a home in Spain." His manner gave off such peacefulness. I felt truly blessed, embraced by that incredible, almost impossible feeling of his warmth and love.

**Strong, simple iron work set into the deep stone windows
of the church at Grañon.**

That was the way it should be: a simple meal, sleeping on the floor packed in like sardines, and the atmosphere of unconditional acceptance and hospitality. This place had the most primitive conditions we had encountered; yet I felt completely at peace and slept like a baby. I think Jesus would have approved.

Grañon to Tosantos
30,034 Steps, 12.8 Miles
April 16

We had been instructed last night not to get up or make any noise before seven in the morning. Hallelujah, our prayers had been answered. No zippers or plastic bag rustled at five o'clock, allowing us to sleep in. Of course, I woke a touch early and had a few quiet moments to meditate on our journey. I determined to drink more water and less wine. Last night I had dreamed blissfully of mailing my entire pack to Santiago and continuing along lightly with only my credit card. It was pathetic that my dreams had degenerated to that level. Even though I hated everything I owned, it was quite unrealistic to fantasize about those things.

We started out at eight in soft early morning light, passing through small villages and miles of vast wheat fields. We walked with a German man named Andrew, who began the day by turning the metal yellow arrow, pointing pilgrims traveling to Santiago the wrong way. His action shocked us after such a kind, embracing stay, yet we still found it hilarious. When a whole group set off in the wrong direction, we were so surprised that we could not even find our voices to stop them. Recovering moments too late, we commented on his bad behavior. Irreverently he said with a laugh, "It is tempting to sin when you will get them all forgiven upon arrival in Santiago." We reminded him that he had not yet arrived, and indeed, he still had quite some distance to travel. However, his theory did have merit if you truly believe you can intentionally do the wrong thing and have your slate wiped clean with a single act of contrition. Terttu suggested that perhaps we should ramp up the sin meter while we still had time.

I thought Andrew looked like a pirate with his black and white Buff worn like a hat/bandana combination tied around his head, his earring, and his beard. Terttu thought he resembled Santa Claus because of his smiling eyes and jolly laugh. Really, who would have known better than Terttu? She claimed that Santa lives in Finland and she worked for him. I knew she looked familiar, the little elf! We stopped a few hours later for a picnic of oranges, apples, bread, cheese, and salami near a fountain in a tiny park. Hungry kittens and puppies immediately surrounded us, begging for food then elusively darting out of petting range. Meanwhile, Andrew was telling us a story, and I asked, "Is that true?" He acted insulted and said, "Yes, of course, it is true. Why would you doubt me?" Terttu immediately said he lacked credibility outside of the fantasy world, as a Santa Claus/pirate persona who sent faithful pilgrims the wrong way to Santiago.

As we continued through farms and villages, Terttu told us of her heartbreaking divorce from her very handsome but unfaithful husband. He obviously was not as intelligent as Scandinavian men are reported to be, or he would not have risked losing someone as lovely as Terttu. She thought it would be a fine experiment to look for a much nicer, less attractive man. Ugly men of the world take heart: one of Santa's favorite elves is looking for you! If you are interested in meeting this magical soul, you may submit a full-disclosure, intellectually stimulating résumé with your ugliest possible photo attached. Post all entries to: Terttu, Santa's Helper, Date-an-Elf Project, Korvatunturi, Finland. If you are selected, she may appear in your life soon. However, please be advised that she will be in disguise, so you must be on your best, most kind behavior with all women you meet this year. And do remember she knows if you have been naughty or nice!

We arrived at Tosantos to find another unique situation at the San Francisco de Assisi parish hostel. The private house, over three hundred years old, had historically served as a pilgrims' hospital and was built on the site of a much older one so continued a long tradition. The owners welcomed people with open arms, and their hostel reflected their warmth. The cheerful yellow house had bright pink trim. Inside, the worn but burnished floors softly glowed against the white walls. And the low ceilings had exquisitely twisted, exposed, dark coffee-colored, wooden beams. We again slept on the floor on mats, in a room that held ten women and had a pink window overlooking the garden. Fresh spring flowers decorated the tables and the hallway. It felt peaceful, a moment stolen from an earlier time.

A funny, handsome French volunteer named Taki warmly welcomed us, along with a kind Spaniard from Madrid named José. We hung our laundry out to dry in the sunshine and were immediately summoned to the kitchen for coffee. A fellow pilgrim taught us a traditional song of the Camino as we drank coffee crowded around the small table. He was very flamboyant, a huge man, sporting a full head of white hair and a beard. He serenaded us, accompanying himself with a bamboo stick/instrument to keep a fanciful rhythm. The song went like this:

Acogenos, Señor Santiago, acogenos.
Acogenos, Señor Santiago, acogenos
En el Camino a Compostela.
Señor Santiago, acogenos.

Welcome us, Mr. Santiago, welcome us.
Welcome us, Mr. Santiago, welcome us
On the road to Compostela.
Mr. Santiago, welcome us.

Then we made up a tale of the Camino and sang it, repeating the above chorus. It can go on for as long as you make up verses. I think he lived on the Camino full time and taught his song to other pilgrims.

We all gathered for a walk up the mountain to visit the Church of our Lady of the Rock, or the Ermita de la Virgen de la Pena, built into the face of the cliffs. It was surrounded by the remains of other caves, where pilgrims bound for Santiago once took shelter. The church dated from the twelfth century, and the walls and ceiling followed the natural lines of the original cave in some places. Within, it holds many statues and a gold altar, with fresh flowers and candles adding to the mystique of this special place. The story goes that the Virgin appeared on the hill with bells on her head and feet. The church was built on the

The 12th century "Our Lady of the Rock" church above the town of Tosantos, and the San Francisco de Asisi pilgrim's hostal.

site of this miracle, and every year, the town has a huge fiesta celebrating her appearance. On May 8 the local people take the statue of the Virgin down to the church in the town below where it stays until mid September. Mystery cloaks the story, and it is vague on many points. However, so much of life is an act of faith. Either you believe something or you don't, and it does not have to make sense to anyone else. The little church was beautiful inside, and you could tell that the people there were very proud. They loved their ritual celebrating this miracle. Who am I to say that their belief itself is not a miracle?

Upon our return to the house, we prepared a communal dinner, supervised by José. For some reason, he chose me to make the main dish, paella. I stirred and sautéed garlic, red and green peppers, chicken, onions, and tomato paste for several hours. Everyone had a job, most chopping ingredients, but Tannis had to measure twenty-two cups of rice and sixty cups of water. All the ingredients were combined, along with bullion cubes and peas. That was one monster pan of paella! I thought I was going to die it smelled so good, and I was so hungry. The Korean women begged a piece of bread, and we all followed suit. I was instructed not to put the rice in until exactly 8:05. (Slobber, slobber, stomach growl.) It turned out fantastic, and I learned how to make real Spanish paella for fifty people. We managed to eat the entire batch with no problem.

After dinner we went to the top floor of the house and had a spiritual gathering. We began by removing our shoes and bowing low to go through a tiny door as a symbol of humility. After two minutes of silence, we sang songs and said personal prayers in many languages, surrounded by the soft glow of candlelight. We read out loud the prayers in many languages left by pilgrims twenty-one days ago. They should have been arriving in Santiago by then. Reading the prayers aloud made them feel tangible and real and gave them a powerful poignancy. I felt connected to the pilgrims who had left something so personal for us yet also carried the prayers to Santiago in their hearts. It bridged a gap of people from across the globe in an amazing experience of the spirit and transmitted an incredible feeling of peace and love.

Tosantos to Agés
30,919 Steps, 13.17 Miles
April 17

The lights went on at 7:15, and Tannis started a riot by looking out the window and declaring it had snowed. Cries of dismay erupted in five languages. The good news was that we would be wearing everything we owned, so our packs would be lighter. As it turned out, it had not actually snowed, but it was cold enough to have, and a very heavy frost covered the ground.

After breakfast, we received a special good-bye from our hosts. José looked at us through warm chocolate-brown eyes with an intensity that seemed to see all the way into our hearts and thanked God for bringing us to this house. I had tears in my eyes as he and Taki hugged us in farewell. They both were so genuine, and caring oozed out of them to form a warm and encompassing environment. The sense of peace they created defied explanation, but I carried it forward with me. Sadly I thought how I would probably never see either one of them again, yet I felt inspired in seeing how one person can touch a life briefly and perhaps change it forever.

I wrote a prayer for my son, Justin, and put it in the box to be given a voice twenty-one days from now by fellow travelers. He has had diabetes since he was seven years old and was not doing so well then. I prayed for his life and for a miracle.

And I cried.

I cried all the way to the next village. I cried for what might have been and for a childhood stolen by needles and bleeding little fingers. How brave my son was, and how responsible he had to be. I remembered standing in the grocery store, feeling overwhelmed, and saying, "There is nothing he can eat here. I cannot do this." My mother, who had come to support me, said, "Yes you can; you have to." That very afternoon he came home from school holding a cupcake. All the other students had eaten their cupcakes in a birthday celebration, and he gave it to me, saying, "I knew I couldn't have it so I brought it home for you." It highlighted the difficulties he would face for the rest of his life in having to evaluate every bite of food and every drink he took and have the will power to refuse each one if it would elevate his blood sugar. I vowed to him that from that moment onward, if he could not eat it, I would not eat it. We made a pact, and we never broke it. Then we split the cupcake and gave him an insulin injection. I promised him I would never use his diabetes as an excuse that he could not do whatever he wanted to do, as long as he wouldn't use it as an excuse to limit himself. Then my husband and I spent the next fifteen years at every sporting game and practice. I volunteered for every school field trip and event. I made sure that if he ever had trouble one of us would be there. We made our lives as a family as good as we could, living well in each moment. Knowing that complications could arise, we still tried not to let his diabetes be the focus of our universe. We learned that even if we did everything perfectly, we would sometimes get terrible results. During one particularly horrible phase, we thought we might loose him despite all our efforts. We decided to try an insulin pump. Justin looked at me with his big brown eyes and said, "I'm scared but I'll try it because I don't want to be blind." Just when you think your heart cannot break again, it does. I told him that I did not want that either. Insulin pumps were new for use with children then. The child wore a suicide machine on his belt all the time in the form of the pump that he controlled to give him the correct dosage of insulin. Bad math in figuring out a dose, multiple times per day, could lead to lowering the blood sugar so much that seizures or diabetic coma ensued. This could spell disaster. However, we trusted Justin's judgment, and it seemed that we had run out of other options. Sometimes you just have to take that leap of faith and believe everything will be fine. I knew that I was a stronger person and that our family was close in ways that we would not have been without this, but I still ached inside. This was not the path I would have chosen for my only child, or for anyone's child. I sometimes got a break from it on trips like this, yet sadly Justin would never get a break. In the end, all any of us can do is our very best, then simply walk on. Each day is new, and we just have to start over again, doing as well as humanly possible, and forgive ourselves for our imperfections.

The weather made travel very tough going that day. An icy headwind was blowing at least thirty miles per hour, so strongly that we had to lean into it just to stay upright. We stopped at a bar for café con leche at the town of Villa Franca Montes de Oca. A man at the bar studied us in surprise and told us we were "*mas fuerte*," or very strong, for being out walking on such a stormy day. He cheered us as we set off with "*contra de viento!*" meaning "into the wind!" Out of town, the way was very steep, a killer climb into gale-force winds. We entered dark, sinister-looking pine forests with a red, sucking mud slick for a road. An intense sleet and hailstorm raged, and we hoped that the mountain cats and wolves that inhabited those woods were snugly tucked into their dens rather than lurking in the forest stalking us. We passed the Korean women, huddled under their ponchos, looking as miserable as we felt. Naturally, as a native of Finland, Terttu felt right at home. Her cheeks were rosy and her laughing smile lit her beautiful face.

At San Juan de Ortega, we made our third stop for nourishment. We got huge bocadillas that amounted to a four-egg omelet filled with ham and cheese on a whole loaf of heavy, crusty bread. Convincing ourselves that we needed this much food to replenish our strength, we inhaled them despite the fact that we could not even get our mouths around them. We decided to test the theory that if we continually ate, drank, and exercised, our metabolisms would speed up, and we would be thin forever. On that philosophical note, we waddled out of the bar and resumed our battle with the elements.

As we broke out into wide-open hills, the weather alternated between dark hailstorms and sudden shifts to blue skies, sunshine, and white fluffy clouds. Toward the end of the day, we were so tired we thought we could not lift our boots one more step. A massive dark gray storm developed with rain coming down in sheets on the nearby hills. Then the lightning and thunder began with a vengeance. We practically ran the last four kilometers into Ages to avoid being fried to a crisp by the lightning that was right over our heads and striking the ground very near us.

We were tired but grateful to find a beautiful albergue and collapsed in a nap. Only utter exhaustion allowed me to ignore the evil

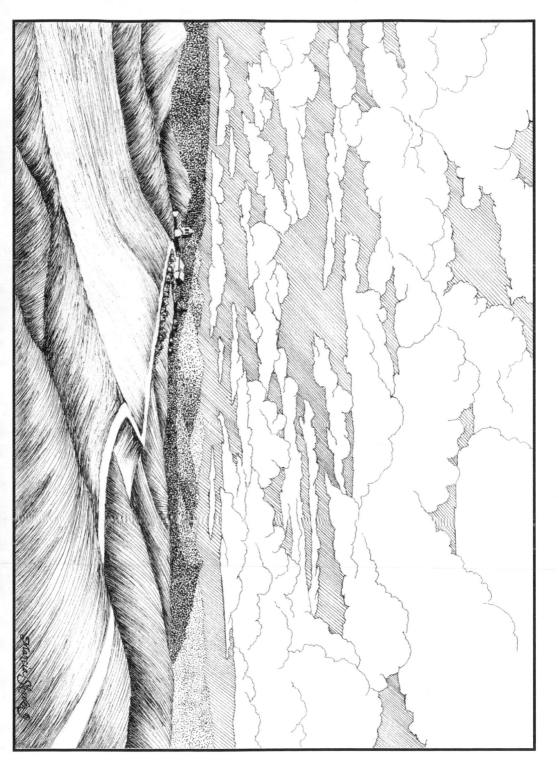

Clouds over the Rioja region near Agés

elves that seemed to be taking sadistic pleasure in beating my legs and feet with a hammer!

Revived by our nap, we ventured downstairs to find a bottle of wine and the most handsome young *peregrino*, Paulo. We had met Paulo in Grañon, and I noticed what a kind, open, spiritual aura he seemed to have. Fantastically multi-lingual, he had worked so hard translating everything for us in the past few days. In Tosantos, he had translated the story of "Ermita de la Virgen de la Peña" (the Shrine of theVirgin of the Rock) for us, or we would not have known anything that the señora was saying. He had also bridged the language barrier with José and Taki to allow us to experience more fully those amazing, spiritual human beings. He was very sensitive when translating parts that seemed extremely personal to fellow pilgrims, allowing them not to feel self-conscious. We invited him to share our wine and found him most pleasant and engaging. His parents were Spanish, and he was raised in France. He had studied in Paris and now worked as a designer in the American film industry. As glamorous as his job sounded, Paulo seemed like a normal, down-to-earth type of young man and a very decent person. We had known him only for a few days, and we would most likely never hear from him again. We were old enough to have been his mother and had little in common except the Camino. Yet he was one of my favorite people that I met on the Camino, however briefly our paths crossed. Kindness and compassion matter.

In another lifetime, his education and career would have been my dream. It is hard to imagine now, but without the Internet, your choices were much more limited. If you lived in a rural community you would never learn about opportunities like that unless someone knew about them personally and told you. What a different direction my life might have taken if those options had existed for me. However, I would not wish away the life I have made for myself or the people I have known. When we are young, we can barely conceptualize that, at each crossroads we come to, our decision on the path chosen can affect the rest of our lives in a major way. Our children would not have existed, we would not have known our friends, we would have different jobs and different spouses, and we would have been part of different communities.

Agés to Burgos
28,869 Steps, 12.3 Miles
April 18

We woke up to the Korean women trying to be quiet but making a huge amount of noise with their plastic-bag rustling. Downstairs we found last night's wineglasses and bottles. Dry sliced bread and cold coffee in thermos bottles to be heated in the microwave consisted of our breakfast. Such a deal for only three euros! That set the tone for the day.

We set out in a whistling wind so strong we could barely stand up, enhanced by driving rain and intermittent hail. We walked all day in our full rain gear with ski hats, gloves, and our Buffs worn like a mask over our faces bandita style to protect us from the elements. We reached the tiny town of Atapuerca in just thirty minutes. Here the archaeological dig had discovered the remains of a new species of our human ancestors eight hundred thousand years old, the oldest in Europe. Just recently the scientists found "anatomical evidence of the hominids that fabricated tools more than one million years ago," which may be the earliest West European hominid. It is chilling to think of people inhabiting these hills and valleys for so many millennia. These were the first people of Europe, perhaps the ancestors of the great cave painters to the north at Altamira who left sophisticated, dynamic art for us to admire and wonder about over fourteen thousand years later. Just walking the same land as these remote humans was eerily fascinating.

We climbed a steep, rocky mountain to find a round maze made of stones laid on the hilltop. There we met Jaime, the local shepherd in his Mitsubishi pick-up. He had a huge flock of sheep that poured over the hills in a white wave, driven by his hard-working German shepherd. After we crested the hill, we could see Burgos far in the distance. We could also see even more ominous weather and black skies although we had our share of the storm close at hand. The wind

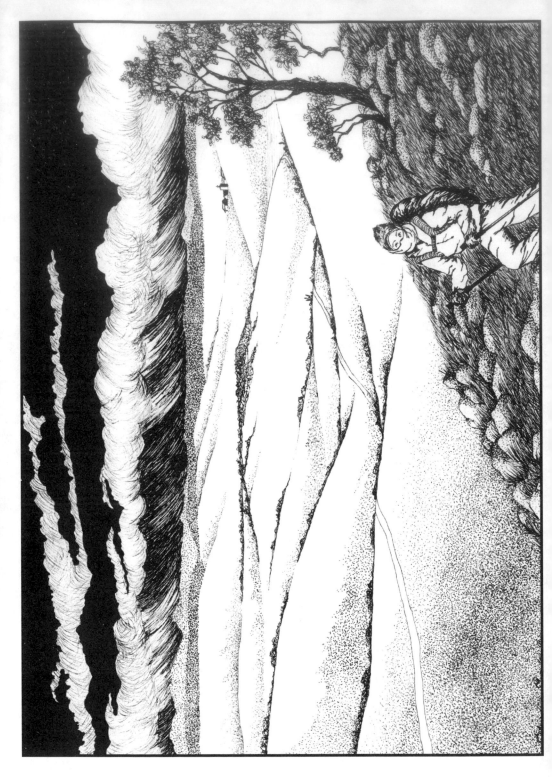

"Into the wind" approaching Burgos

blasted fierce and cold, literally blowing the rain cover on Tannis's pack away. She searched for it in vain as we fell far behind Terttu. By the time we reached the village of Riopico, or the first bar, we were a good imitation of a Popsicle. Our pilgrim friend Paulo told us we had just missed Terttu, so we had a very quick café and forged on to the next town. We still did not catch up with Terttu as she was walking as fast as she could to stave off the cold. We opted for the shorter and less scenic route into Burgos because it was so foggy we could not see anything. I commented that it did not even feel safe to be out in that weather. Just then, the wind picked up, howling in excess of a hundred kilometers, or sixty miles, per hour. Driving sleet and hail surrounded us, and the gale nearly blew us off the road. The road had no protecting shoulder, only a steep drop off on each side. We were soaked all the way to the bone, with the wind blowing the rain up our pants' legs and down our backs. Water filled my boots, and my feet were drenched. We could only see about three feet in front of us, and as luck would have it, there was not one yellow arrow in sight. For the first—and only—time in my life, the wind blew the snot right out of my nose and away to an unknown destination. Finally, we sighted a bridge into the aptly named village of Villafría (cold town). Ugly industrial sprawl had never in our lives looked so inviting! It had been the slog of a lifetime. We went into the nearest bar and found two German women, equally drenched, plotting to take Autobus Numero Ocho. We joined them, and by the time we hit Burgos centro, I was shaking so hard I could not hold my trekking poles. I just let them dangle from the straps and drag along beside me. We doggedly found the Tourist Office. *CERRADO!* I felt like kicking the door in. What kind of a country closes the Tourist Office all afternoon just when it is needed? We were standing in front of a World Heritage site, one of the most beautiful cathedrals in the world, and all I could think was, "Who the blank cares?" Dejectedly we left and finally found a nice hotel. Hypothermic, I indulged in a hot bubble bath and felt certain that I had died and gone to heaven.

We later learned that we had lost our wonderful, funny, beautiful friend, Terttu, in the storm near Villafría, just before Burgos. She became so chilled waiting for us in a café that she had to move on and walk fast to keep up her body heat. She had looked for us in the cathedral, but somehow we had missed each other. She said later in an email, "That is life. We meet and have our time. After those good moments we shared, we are stronger and happier to continue on our separate ways. God bless you both." We would never catch up with Terttu again, but her mischievous spirit and fun loving ways would always bring a smile to my heart. Her courage in taking a year to learn to be alone, laughing and making new friends instead of getting depressed following a terrible experience was so admirable. What a cheerful, strong, amazing woman we had the good fortune to meet. She was a survivor, battling through the darkness to reach a happier place within herself. Imagine that: fantastic people, hailing from lands we have never before dreamed of, can join us on our journey and lighten our load as they share with us their joy.

Incredibly, after we got warm and dry, we actually rallied and went out into town. At the now open Tourist Office, we got a map and found out where the post office, or *correos*, was located. We bought a much too-small box to ship unnecessary items on to Santiago, a pair of black plastic shoes, and some thin socks for me. We returned to the hotel to select items to get rid of. My pile included tennis shoes and sandals, which I had not been able to get my swollen feet into since the fourth day. In their place, my new *zapatos palstico* (plastic shoes) felt very comfortable and weighed nothing. I sent my silk sleep sack because I did not need both it and the sleeping bag. Both my skirts went because we had thought it would be ninety degrees on the *meseta*, the high plain occupying the center portion of the Camino. We had reached the edge of the meseta; it was literally freezing, and later we would go into the mountains again. All of my first aid supplies went, with the exception of a needle, tape, and Compeed to treat my blisters. True artist to the core, I kept my sketchbook, pens, and pencil, altogether weighing two and a half pounds. I got really brutal with my remaining selections. Even though they weighed only ounces each, all added up to six pounds. Was this symbolic of the weight and responsibility of possessions we carry in our every day lives, which are not necessary? Do we own our possessions, or do they own us? We would mail our packages to Santiago tomorrow with a prayer and a sigh. Would it be in Santiago when we arrived? What would happen to it if we did not reach Santiago? How long did they store "pilgrim packages" before finally discarding them? We had carried the extra burden a third of the journey and felt great glee at finally downloading even the smallest amount of excess weight. Our packs were much lighter, and we noticed the reduced strain on our knees and feet. Feeling very smug about the things we could do without, we found a very fashionable tapas bar and gorged ourselves.

Burgos
10,526 Steps, 4.48 Miles
April 19

I had a "Princess and the Pea" night in Burgos. My feet smelled as if they had died, so I took the shoe cleaner/buffer thing from the hotel and scrubbed them. Trying not to fret that they were getting gangrene from being so swollen, I cut my toenails and lusted after some pink nail polish. However, by the time I had finished shining them up, even the purple was kind of a nice hue. A little squirt of Chanel #5, and the Perfumed Pilgrim was ready for a luxurious bed and a good night's sleep. But *no*! The bed was too comfortable. It was so quiet you could hear a pin drop. It was warm. I could *not* sleep. The first time in a month that I had real sheets, and it hurt to have them touch my toes. Apparently, I had been over zealous in my scrubbing. And my calves tightened up so much that my ankles welded into right angles. When I tried to straighten them out and point my toes, I could not. I gave up and rolled onto my stomach, hanging my petrified right-angle feet off the end of the bed. Then my feet got cold, but I was too lazy to do anything about it. Next I fixated on not knowing what time it was because I had packed my cute little alarm clock in the "To Go to Santiago" box. Sigh! Meanwhile, "she who has trouble sleeping" was out like a light until seven thirty in the morning.

We had a very nice day, much due to the fact that we were inside, cleverly, as the rain and wind continued. The Burgos Museum was located in two fabulous houses, which were constructed in the 1200s. It encompassed the history, artifacts, and art of that specific region. Beginning with the archaeological digs at Atapuerca, the extensive collection continued with coins, sculpture, and intricate mosaics from the Roman city of Clunia, which was located near present day Burgos. Later works from the Middle Ages and Renaissance gave us the sense of how much had happened over the millennia in this very spot. There were entire sections of sculpted tombs, chapels, and altars out of various monasteries and churches. Within that fantastic museum, we had almost the whole place to ourselves.

We took a great recommendation for lunch and had the *menu del dia*, or daily special, surrounded by walls of deep blue multi-layered glazing. We lunched until three o'clock and were so satiated we nearly decided to go native and indulge in a siesta. But we were strong and pushed onward as we had not yet seen most of the town.

Situated in the middle of the high plains of Old Castile, Burgos was a Spanish crossroads for thousands of years. Traversed by the ancient people native to this region, this area later became an important Roman outpost. Burgos itself was founded in 844 as a fortification against Islamic invaders. Many of the landmarks had to do with its beloved native son, El Cid, a warrior instrumental in the defeat of the Moors in the Christian re-conquest of Spain. The cathedral was begun in 1221 and has been holding services since 1230. It dominated the town in its sheer magnitude and beauty, and is one of Spain's greatest Gothic cathedrals. Although it had been added on to over the centuries, it retained a cohesive feeling. Surprisingly, a large star-of-David stained glass window looked over one of the entrances to the cathedral. It also had sections that clearly showed the influence of Muslim architectural elements. During the centuries that the Moors ruled Spain, the society practiced a tolerant "separate but equal" concept of living together. An entire art form developed in the twelfth to sixteenth centuries to reflect this blending of the cultures, known as Mudéjar. It incorporated design elements from the Muslim, Jewish, and Christian faiths, fusing them into a unique and distinctive style. Its richness and complexity manifests life in our diverse world. What a gift we would give to mankind if we could find a way to live side by side and assimilate the good parts of our many cultures, just as the artists of the Mudéjar style blended various design elements to create works of beauty.

The floors of the cathedral consisted of wonderful patterns made of huge pieces of black and cream stone arranged in squares, diagonals, rectangles, and triangles. The interior was truly exquisite with its white-on-white, intricately sculpted stone. Although gold decorated the cathedral, the pure, clean stonework gave a far greater impression. It looked like delicate lace, and as I marveled at its beauty, I wondered how it stood up structurally. It seemed to be constructed of thin air, with a few stone supports thrown in. As we looked up into the central vaults, a warm light fell softly through the star-shaped stone lace, filtering down to encompass us in its glow. It was as if a window to heaven had opened.

As we were leaving the cathedral, we came to a long rib-vaulted hallway with stained glass windows. The sun filtering through the glass cast a warm glow of rose, green, russet, blue, and gold onto the stone flooring. The colored light danced on the air and settled on the walls and floors, mirroring the patterns of the intensely stained windows.

Fortress-like walls embraced the plaza surrounding the cathedral with all of the fanfare and decoration worthy of a castle. Against this ancient architecture, the juxtaposition of huge modern sculptures leading to the entryway managed to work aesthetically and please our artistic senses. Long running archways of plane trees braided together added the final touch of elegance to the old center of this city sitting at the edge of the meseta. Tomorrow would bring a new region. I was proud of us for making it this far and daunted by another two thirds of the journey to go. "Ready or not, here we come!"

The light filled Burgos cathedral cloister

Burgos to Hontanas
29,280 Steps, 12.5 Miles
April 20

This morning we met a fellow American from our corner of the country. We were having a quiet breakfast after a lazy lie-in until eight thirty. The woman entered the hotel bar terribly loudly and began complaining about everything. She was frantic because she had checked the Internet and found that it was snowing in Leon, and the current weather was supposed to be wretched. So what if there was snow in Leon? Leon was ten days' walk from Burgos, and by the time we would arrive the weather would have changed. Talk about freaking yourself out with too much information! She had taken a taxi with two Spanish men from the "suburbs," Atapuerca, which was twenty miles away and could hardly be considered the suburbs. She thought she would go to Madrid for a few days, pick up an art print, possibly go to the south of Spain for some sunshine, then fly to Leon and begin again.

She seemed to me a pampered woman with a lot of money. Her words and actions said she wanted to walk the Camino because it would impress others and not because she would grow as a person. She was searching for any and all reasons to abandon her Camino because she did not truly want to be there. She was trying to find an excuse to quit and use the "poor me" scenario. She had found one, and she would probably find another and then another until quitting would become the right thing to do. Her hysterical attitude really had a negative effect on me. I had such a difficult time putting on my rain gear and starting the walk again. My indirect encounter with her provided a prime example of how continually exposing ourselves to negative people and situations and listening to or reading depressing accounts can put us into a downward spiral. I felt as if she was a messenger sent to tell me to keep going, stay focused, and not give up.

Much to our surprise, we saw the same woman two and a half weeks later at Samos Monastery while we were having a quiet lunch on a park bench. She flitted up to us, informing us loudly that she had already been to Santiago, having walked from Triacastela. She had then walked on to Finisterre, had been to Madrid twice, and had returned to Burgos to walk one day to Hontanas so that she could experience the meseta. Now she had returned to Samos via bus because it was her favorite place. She told us how her pack no longer felt heavy now that she had been walking continuously for thirty days. Next she lectured us on how the rest of our Camino should be done and what we absolutely had to see. It was the most hyperactive, disjointed conversation I have ever had. It was impossible to have done what she was claiming. What she said did not make sense, and the days did not add up. When asked for details, she was very vague and nervous.

I had to wonder why she was being untruthful with herself as well as with us. Who was she trying to convince? She did not walk any stretch of the Camino for more than a couple of days. She had train, bus, taxi, airplane, hotel, and restaurant stories. She did not have walking stories, or people stories. I felt so very sorry for her because she only pretended to walk the Camino de Santiago, and she had squandered a great opportunity. By visiting a few places along the way, in her mind, she believed she had walked it. However, it was a false Camino. How sad to have deluded herself and been completely out of touch with the true spirit of the Camino. She never got to slow down and experience the continuity of traversing the countryside on foot. She missed meeting people from all over the world and bonding with them through food, wine, laughter, hard floors, and stormy weather. She did not test her resolve and find herself stronger. She did not examine her faith or find new corners of her heart. I had the sad feeling that she had missed the greatest adventure of her life.

Tannis and I agreed not to let negative thoughts intimidate us from setting out that day. What could be worse than the storm we had walked in two days ago? We took a taxi to the outskirts of Burgos and began our walk near Tarjados on a golden pathway lit by early morning sunshine. We soon came to a panadería and bought a huge, flat, round loaf of bread for our picnic. The warm, yeasty aroma enveloped us and perfumed the air as we stepped into a new region, the meseta. The saying goes that there you have "nine months of winter and three months of hell." It was a high plateau standing at 2100' to 3000', surrounded by mountains, with few trees. During the Christian re-conquest of Spain, it was deforested. One had to wonder if the native trees built the Spanish Armada, which immediately went to the bottom of the sea. The area was the heart of Old Castile, from which sprang the culture and language that would go on to dominate much of the world. These fertile plains have served as the breadbasket to many countries since Roman times, when retired legionaries were granted land to grow wheat.

The meseta was not flat! We traversed rolling hills with many grayish white stones, some set in large piles and others made into fences. The sky loomed large over the endlessly undulating land, low on the horizon. The fantastic expanse of sky dominated all, giving a clean, open, free feeling where you could see unimpaired for great distances. It had its own quiet beauty. We had wonderful weather for walking with only periods of rain, sleet, and hail. Some of the tracks of road had turned into small lakes, and even the puddles had whitecaps! The track was very muddy, and I almost lost my boot in one spot as the red goo turned into a sucking vortex. Tempestuous storms swirled around us, then completely disappeared. However, the changing weather made the skies and clouds very dramatic. When the sun shone, the landscape sparkled, and it was really a perfect temperature. I was so thankful that we had not been frightened off the trail or just too lazy to go out because it had looked miserable from our nice, warm hotel. We would have missed a beautiful and dramatic day. It felt good to be back walking, and our resolve to continue and finish was strengthened.

Since the clearing of the forests, the wind has been an ever-present and prominent feature of the meseta. The towns were built tucked down into the belly of the hills to seek protection from the relentless gusts. As we walked, we felt as if there were no buildings as far as the eye could see. Suddenly, we would drop into a swale, and the rooftops of a medieval village would appear. Late in the afternoon, as it began to hail in earnest, we dropped down into the welcoming village of Hontanas. Safe, secure, and warm in our albergue, we drew the ancient-looking tile roofs from the lovely upstairs room.

Rooftops of Hontanas

Hontanas to Itero de la Vega
29,858 Steps, 12.72 Miles
April 21

Last night we met a French man who was very inebriated. After a beautiful dinner, he made a huge scene about us being Americans. He asked to see our passports and jovially insisted on buying us a cognac. Not wanting to drink cognac, but also not wanting to offend a friendly person, we accepted. He immediately and loudly proclaimed, "I love George Bush!" Of course we suspected this was a lie even before he reversed his statement with a profanity because most Europeans did not approve of President Bush. That brought up the uneasy question of what he truly thought of us as Americans. He spent the next twenty minutes telling me I looked like a certain movie star, trying to cop a feel, and singing the American national anthem. I was old enough to know better than to believe his intentions were sincere, but I felt young enough to be flattered and appreciate the lie! He made us feel exceedingly uncomfortable. In a show of international solidarity, all the other pilgrims were glaring at him and giving us ruefully supportive glances. We escaped out the front door, then snuck back inside, and made our way to our room without being seen. The lights were out and our three roommates were already sleeping.

The Frenchman burst into several of the rooms, including ours, numerous times as he sang, shouted, and looked for us. We had buried our heads in the pillows and pretended to be asleep. Sometimes it is so hard to be a goddess. Eventually the señora threw him out, and he had to sleep in the expensive hotel down the road. This morning, I invited two hulking, tank-like Germans to share my table for coffee. When I heard the Frenchman's voice, I tried to ignore him, surrounded by my three-hundred-pound German bodyguards, but he lingered anyway. When I glanced up, he looked sheepish and sober. He shook my hand, and I said it was OK, then continued to ignore him. My bodyguards scowled fiercely and patted my hand protectively. They considered breaking him in half as he had kept them awake last night as well. He slipped away, and I noticed that he was wearing sandals. He approached the señora, saying he had forgotten his boots last night. The boots had mysteriously vanished and could not be found. It was such perfect justice that he had to walk in sandals in freezing rain and mud because he had been so naughty last night. Ah-ha! The cosmic energy of the Camino had struck again.

We set off from the lovely little medieval town of Hontanas in the cool, crisp morning air. The blue sky overhead was filled with layers of dramatic cloud formations. We wound our way along the base of hills, following the contours of the land. The hillsides tumbled down to meet the valley floor. Stone fences punctuated the landscape, and poplar trees lined the streams. We came upon a spectacular ruin of the Convento San Anton. Its huge golden vaults spanned the road and stood silhouetted against the clear blue Spanish sky. It had been a medieval pilgrims' hospital and was the site of a miracle cure for San Anton's fire, a burning disease similar to leprosy. The convent must have been huge in its day, and now stands as a silent reminder of all those that trod these pathways to Santiago before us.

We passed under the arches and walked onward through green fields and wild lavender. Wildflowers dusted the pathway with their brilliant colors. As we rounded a corner, a huge symmetrical hill with a dramatic castle ruin on top appeared before us. A village and a fantastic church complex skirted the hill. It was the town of Castrojerez. The hill had Celtiberian origins, and you could almost see a beautiful structure underneath the even slope of the hill. Today it is laced with caves, called *bodegas*, in which the local wine and mushroom harvest are stored.

We had an early picnic in the sunny windbreak of the ruins of Iglesia de Santa Maria as birds serenaded us. This seventy-degree day was a miracle after the extreme wind, sleet, hail, and mud we had so recently experienced.

As we walked across the valley, we traveled on an elevated Roman road built to allow passage over the boggy land. It was raised about four feet, perfectly straight, and supported by hundreds of small arches made of stone. There were Roman gold mines in this area, and either

Caesar or Pompey supposedly founded the ruined castle. But archaeologists date it to much earlier origins, as if two thousand years is not old enough! It was astonishing to visualize the Celtiberians, Romans, Visigoths, Muslims, and later the crusading Christians all occupying the high ground of that castle. It must have had a great view to be worthy all of that conquering!

We climbed straight up to the Alto de Mostelares, panting and having flashbacks to the Route Napoleon over the Pyrenees. At one point, a yellow arrow pointed straight up to the sky, which we thought was either a cruel joke or just plain WRONG! I whined "*Flecha amarilla es muy mal*" (the yellow arrow is very bad), and representatives from five continents snorted in agreement. It was all we could manage, as none of us could breathe normally enough actually to laugh. We finally reached the summit to find very strong winds and a changing sky. Steeply downhill, a mirror of what we had just climbed, we saw more wheat fields stretching westward. We walked across a beautiful eleven-arched bridge with the Río Pisuerga flowing very fast and full. We had arrived at our destination, Itero de la Vega.

We passed a very crowded, commercial-looking albergue at the edge of town. We walked into the center of town and found the delightful hostel La Posada. Clean and quiet, it had red bunk beds and only five other people staying there. We did our laundry in the outdoor courtyard with a scrub board and cold water. We reflected that some time ago I started having issues with my underwear. First, I had a fight with my sports bra. I was so tired after a long day of slogging through the mud that I could not get out of it. I thought, "I have to do better than this; I can *not* be this helpless!" But after struggling in vain for a few more minutes, I gave up and slept in it. When I confessed this to Martien, he had the most puzzled look on his face and asked very seriously, "Are zey so tight?" In the morning while it was still dark, I picked my panties and socks off the floor, where I had unceremoniously dropped them, and put them on … **dirty!** Oh my God, I had turned into **a man**! I required not so much as a sniff test! EEEKKK! Laundry had degenerated to a smell and a quick wash of only the offensive areas with a bar of soap in cold water. A clothesline strung between our beds or an open yard served as our dryer. A modern washer and dryer had become a vague memory.

Itero de la Vega is a small village of brick and adobe houses springing from the fertile earth of the meseta. The tiny central plaza has iron benches and is surrounded by the ever-present silvery plane trees. Tannis thought the trees looked tortured, but to me the braided branches formed a welcoming embrace of the plaza. I found them very beautiful in their austerity and graphic simplicity against the ever-changing sky. We drew beneath their sturdy limbs, and a young man named "G" soon joined us. As we drew the trees silhouetted against the blue sky, we heard his story. That amazing young Dutch man, twenty-two years in age, had walked all the way from Amsterdam carrying a sixty-pound pack. He had left Holland in February, and by the time he would arrive in Santiago, he would have walked twenty-eight hundred kilometers, or 1680 miles. Tall and gaunt, with red hair and beard, he is the same age as my son, Justin, and glows with confidence and a positive attitude. He told us that anyone could walk the Camino with willpower. He walked from six in the morning until eight in the evening on that first wintry day. Finding no place to stay, he went into a church. He was so tired and lost that he began to cry as he sat there. The local people took him home to care for him, and fed him. He told us that he had found kindness all along the Camino, through several countries, and that it exists everywhere if only we look for it. He assured us with a forceful smile and a penetrating gaze that we *would* make it all the way to Santiago. His quiet strength was extraordinary. He will carry with him for the rest of his life the knowledge that he can do anything. I told him that his mother and father would not recognize him when they would meet him in Santiago, but they would be very proud of him. He left home a boy and would arrive in Santiago a good and powerful man.

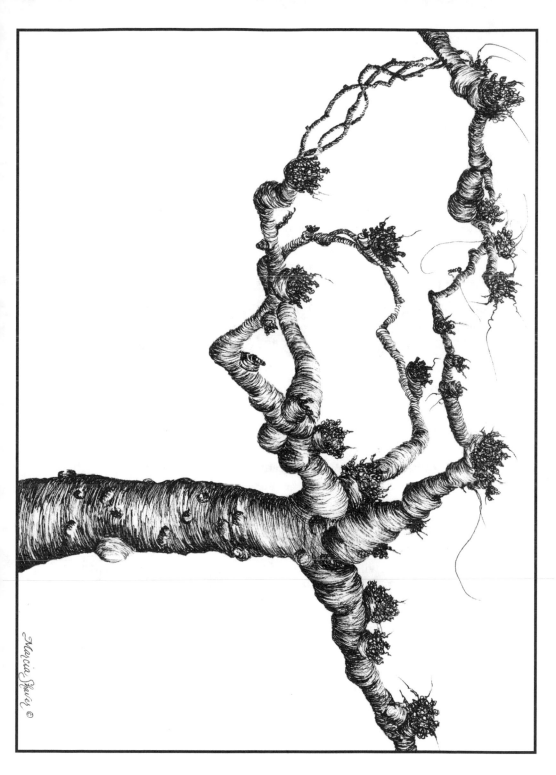

Braided Plane trees

Itero de la Vega to Villalcázar de Sirga
43,229 Steps, 18.39 Miles
April 22

Without coffee, we set off to a pink sunrise and clear skies. We walked uphill very slightly through more verdant fields of new wheat and barley. When we approached the small village of Boadilla del Camino, a cute older man came out to greet us. He stood about five feet tall and wore a formal hat, a red tie, and a jacket with a name tag stating, "Alejandro Dandoval Ortega, Amigo de los Peregrinos," or "friend of the pilgrims." He smiled as he asked us to sign his little notebook, where he collects signatures from around the globe. He went out each morning, offering his sweet welcome, to strangers who instantly became friends. He made it his life to be nice to people and make them feel at home in his little corner of the world.

Soon we entered the town and were met by a young man named Eduardo. He directed us into his family albergue, saying his mama made the best coffee in town. We were delighted to discover that the coffee and a great ham and eggs breakfast were the best ever. The restaurant looked out over a beautiful walled garden with sculptures, tulips, green grass, and brilliantly painted yellow ocher walls. Eduardo had five black German shepherd puppies about two or three months old. They were playing with something that was driving them into a frenzy of gymnastic and entertaining moves. Eduardo told us that it was the cuttings off his horse's feet, which he had trimmed yesterday. I asked him what kind of horses he had, and he said, "THE BEST KIND!" We went out to meet his three horses that were, indeed, beautiful. Gray and white, they had fiery dark eyes and streamlined physiques. Prancing and tossing their heads, they still let us feed them our leftover bread and stroke their silky necks and soft noses. They look like fine-boned horses of Arab descent and could probably run like the wind. I longed to drop my backpack, grab a hand full of mane, and swing onto their backs for a sprint across the plains.

After we left the horses, Eduardo showed us a sixteenth-century tunnel he had discovered under the town that led from the church under his house and onward to somewhere undetermined. He was excavating it, and we got to climb down the ladder to see the exposed stone vaults, which had been built centuries ago, then filled in for reasons unknown.

Eduardo made our short time in Boadilla special and interesting. We enjoyed seeing someone excited about where he lived, especially when some people might have considered it boring, being in the middle of nowhere. I could not imagine skipping the meseta and missing that part of Spain. There we found value beyond the obvious appearances—in relationships of people being just plain nice to each other.

We walked on to Fromista where we took a break and visited the cheese museum across from the beautifully restored eleventh-century Romanesque church of San Martin. The stone was a soft yellow-gold color, shaped into rounded windows and sculpted human and animal forms. It was quite perfect due to extensive restoration, which fueled controversy as to whether it should have been done. However, I think it gave us a glimpse into what all of these churches stretching across Europe had once looked like—lovely.

We decided to push on to Villalcázar de Sirga. But my feet hurt so badly that we stopped at an albergue a couple of miles short of our goal. I flopped on the bunk bed nearly unconscious from fatigue, but Tannis was more aware. She pointed out that it did not appear to be open for the season as dirty dishes sat in the sink, the floors were not swept, the showers were not turned on, and we were the only two people there. I realized that I was lying on dirty sheets from last season, so I had to agree that it did not feel right. We rallied and slipped out the back door, walking another three or four miles along a paved road. Not for the first time, just when I thought I could not possibly go one step further, I discovered I actually could. Every agonizing step was impor- tant and every little centimeter became a goal accomplished. Marching so far, for so many days in a row, had never been just a stroll in the park. However, this day underscored what an arduous trek Tannis and

I had undertaken. We found a strength within ourselves, somewhere deep and hidden.

After that mistaken stop, we welcomed the sight of a clean albergue, a hot shower, and a bed in a quiet room. Still, we were so tired we questioned whether we had arrived at a proper albergue. We must have snapped at Hubert, our Dutch host, who had a round face and a sweet disposition, or acted grumpy, because he got an alarmed look on his face and asked, "Is there a problem?" Tannis said, "No, there is no problem." I added, "We have walked so far and are just so very tired." Kindly, he put us in a special room with nobody else in it. Later a group of three beautiful young Spanish women from the Canary Islands joined us, but the main bedroom was crowded and noisy. I was ashamed of myself for being rude to Hubert, especially because he responded to my rudeness with extra consideration and kindness. Nothing, not even my extreme fatigue, excused my behaving badly to an innocent bystander. His response won my heart and put me in my place so much more effectively than being rude in return ever would have.

Villalcázar de Sirga to Calzadilla de la Cueza
34,105 Steps, 14.5 Miles
April 23

We woke to the cheerful sound of birds singing in the pine tree outside our window. After a good night's sleep and a hearty breakfast, we felt very rejuvenated. We kissed Hubert good-bye on the cheek, and he blushed, saying we would spoil him. We told him there can never be too much love in the world and thanked him for his kindness. He smiled, and said, "You are so right. There can never be too much love." We hugged him and waved as he was preparing to set off on his bicycle to travel to the next town. He was traveling to check on a woman who had been having heart trouble the night before. The ambulance had taken her to the regional hospital for tests and observation. It was so good to know that if a problem arose, the medical care in Spain would be fast, efficient, and professional.

Big skies over the meseta near Villalcázar de Sirga

The church that dominated the town, Santa Maria la Blanca, was built by the Knights Templar in the thirteenth century. The façade held a magnificent rose window, and sculpture richly decorated the portal to the main door. Partially destroyed, the church showed other signs of wear—it had definite cracks in the wall housing the rose window and a disconcerting lean to the left.

The walk to Carrión de los Condes was much flatter, but the early morning light and mists rising off the land created a very ethereal feeling. The trees on the horizon shimmered softly as the birds sang. We crossed medieval bridges and walked on Roman roads for quite some time, level and straight as an arrow. Leading us ever westward, the roads built by the Romans connected France with the mining areas near Astorga. It rained for a little while, but it was mostly a warm, overcast day with tiny yellow birds and wild flowers decorating the way.

The meseta is a wondrous place filled with friendly people, big wide-open skies, serenading birds, and clean and productive farms with the light playing over hills of rippling green wheat. How people consider this boring and unworthy defies comprehension. What a loss for them. You can walk forever on a straight path laid out by the Romans and think good thoughts in the peaceful silence of the Spanish countryside.

We saw the church spire long before we reached our destination in Calzadilla de la Cueza. There we discovered the true meaning of happiness. We sat in the courtyard of our little refugio, basking in the sun with our backs to a warm, yellow ochre wall. Sheltered from the wind, we rested comfortably and gazed upward as the most gorgeous clouds danced in the blue sky. We were drawing in the warm sunshine, playing the childhood game of finding shapes in the clouds. Was that a dragon? No, it just turned into an angel. The angel changed from praying to playing tennis. Wait, that was not an angel; it was a rabbit. Why did we ever abandon this entertaining pastime as adults? Meanwhile, one man was cheerfully doing our laundry, and another man was cooking our dinner. It just could not get any better than that!

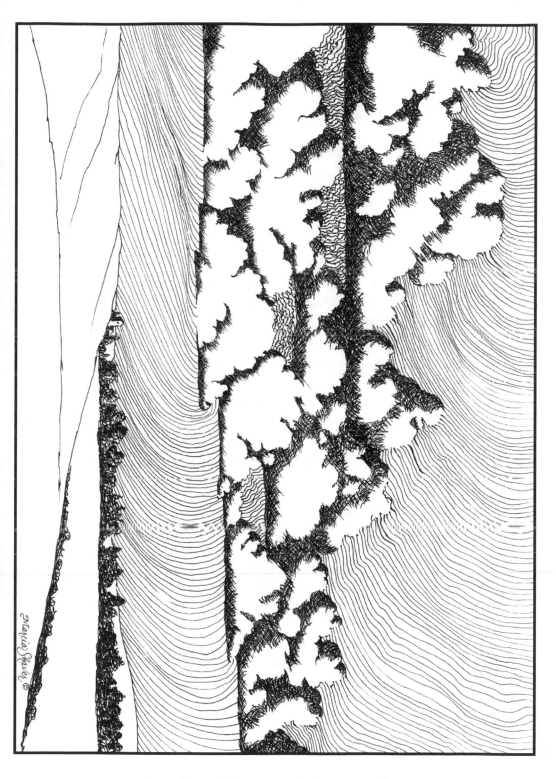

Cloud watching on a windy meseta day.

Calzadilla de La Cueza to Calzada del Coto
38,245 Steps, 16.29 Miles
April 24

Last night I discovered a new international standard for lack of modesty. Not only did the Germans scratch their butts and walk around in their underwear, which by the way we were just getting used to, they also dropped their shorts and changed gymnastically and unselfconsciously into their jammies in a room with thirty people and the lights on. "Jeez, why don´t you just do your yoga stretches naked while you are at it?" That, of course, led to fantasies because I did not know if the equipment belonged to a twenty-year-old or an eighty-year-old. I was contemplating a conjugal flight home, and then someone passed a gigantic amount of gas and spoiled the mood.

This morning, my foreign companions treated me to the reverse German pants dance with a frontal view. Shish! Every time we saw him during the day, he gave us a big smile. "Listen buster, I know what you have in there! Put that Wiener schnitzel away right now. We do *not* want to see it again!" Later in the afternoon, we came over a hill and surprised him with an uncomfortable look on his face as he pulled his pants up hastily. *As if* we had not seen it already! We named him Hans and laughed all the way to the next town.

Truly, laughing at the Germans was like laughing at myself. These were my people, sharing with me an earthy sense of humor and a lack of modesty. When I looked at them, it was like peering into a mirror. I saw myself reflected in people I had never met but who looked like me and just happened to live on a different continent. Genetics must play a huge part in personality traits as well as physical traits.

The skies were pristinely clear, rosy, and full of promise for a beautiful spring day. As the sun rose, it set fire to the deeply plowed red earth and rippling green fields. The meseta was less flat and began to rise and fall again like gentle waves. Purple irises poked their heads up next to walls made of a jumble of stone and broken brick, in an echo of modernist architecture. The dramatic, snow covered Pecos de

Adobe houses and bright flowers spring from the meseta soil

Europa mountains and pine plantations seemed to grow closer, just to the north of our pathway. We passed through villages with yellow ochre adobe walls. Made from the earth and straw, the bricks retained a rich texture. Bright turquoise or cobalt blue doors punctuated the more muted natural colors of the homes, and hundreds of yellow and orange flowers skirted the buildings.

After a few miles, we came to the village of Moratinos with a hill that looked like it was inhabited by Hobbits. We ventured into one of them with a welcoming scallop shell near the door. They were bodegas where the local wine is made and stored in low, vaulted caves. We met Celestino, who served us olives, homemade sausage, and his own wine. He still used the winepress in the cave, which was several hundred years old. An English man named Patrick was there having a sip of wine and translating for us. It was a sweet interlude in Spanish hospitality.

We walked and walked, reaching Calzada del Coto via a freeway overpass at nearly five thirty. Footsore, we limped to the municipal albergue, a tiny, whitewashed, square building in the grassy strip that functioned as the city park. The key was in the door with nobody in attendance. Inside, two rooms, each probably fourteen feet by sixteen feet, contained six bunks (twelve beds) and a tiny table and chairs. There were two clean bathrooms, and a clothesline hung next to the basketball court. We settled in one room, and a quiet, blushing German man named Helmut secured the other. We could not believe we had met another man with that great name that is so much fun to say, so we christened him "Helmut the Second." All that for only a donativo! There are many accommodations along the Camino where you can stay for a donation in whatever amount that you can afford. Many times a meal was also included. We always made it a point to donate the same amount that we would have paid for a bed and a meal at an albergue that charged a set fee. We felt as if we were in the lap of luxury to have a private room. However, it would not have felt overcrowded even if every bunk had been full because the beds were arranged around the whitewashed, immaculately clean walls. It was Spartan, but we needed nothing more. We were exceedingly grateful for a clean, safe place to stay, regardless of how humble it was. It just goes to show you how many people one can house comfortably yet simply and how our priorities had changed. How amazing and wonderful that the tiny farming community provided this place free to pilgrims. The señora in the bar stamped our passports with a smile, fed us a great dinner, and left us coffee in thermoses for the morning. Her husband took care of the park lawn, mowing it as needed. In the quiet of this very simple and wonderful albergue, I felt the spirit of the Camino, alive and well.

Calzada del Coto to Reliegos
37,264 Steps, 15.87 Miles
April 25

We had a long day of walking in the sunshine, mostly parallel to a quiet secondary road. It was another beautiful day on the meseta, and so many birds with enchanting songs that we have not heard before entertained us. Here the land lay flat against the horizon, the slight rises tucked firmly into the earth. Swelling like the sea, the low hills undulated in a gentle rhythm as the sun beat strongly down. The pathway sought out the quiet contours of the land, and the Camino friends had planted trees next to the pathway every fifteen feet for as far as you could see. They were the same kind of trees that were sculpted and braided around the many plazas across Spain, but these were left natural. When they leaf out and grow taller, they will eventually provide a welcome sanctuary on this otherwise open and shade-less traverse. They will be big, untrimmed plane trees, sheltering pilgrims from the relentless meseta sun. Today, bare of leaves, they swayed in the breeze and cast an intricate spider web of shadows across the curving pathway.

We had the oddest experience when we stopped midday for café con leche. We were approached by a very tall Dutch man, named Yampah, which he explained was a spiritual name he had chosen for himself. He had white hair worn on top of his head in a bun and a long white beard. He was dressed strangely in tights with shorts over the top and what appeared to be size sixteen boots. When he found out that we were Americans, he got agitated and told us that Martien was

Plane trees on the road to Reliegos

looking for us. This was not news to us because for days in every town we passed through people said to us, "Oh, you are the two American girls that Martien is searching for." I had just checked email for the first time in ages, and I had four or five messages from Martien in addition to multiple messages from him on my emergency phone. We had treated it like a joke, saying Jacqueline had probably ditched him just as he had thrown us over for her. We had developed a reputation, which proceeded us on the Camino, for being sought after. How delicious!

However, Yampah warned us not to get involved with Martien. Yampah proclaimed that Martien was dangerous and had many problems which he, all too happily, elaborated on. His negative talk made us nervous and gave the entire scenario a sinister feel, as if we were being stalked. As we walked on, I re-centered my thoughts and focused on what I knew intuitively to be true. Not one thing in Martien's behavior would validate Yampah's accusations. I had felt only kindness and an open camaraderie from Martien, who held a kind of boyish enthusiasm for this adventure. It was Yampah that was weird and lonely, stealthily trying to get us on his side by saying bad things about someone else.

How many people do we know that use those tactics, falsely accusing an innocent person? His insidious method made us doubt someone who did not deserve our mistrust, and the doubt tended to linger once he had planted that seed of an idea. In our lives at home, we are often too tired or preoccupied to evaluate clearly and dismiss accusations of a negative nature. Then the more times we hear a rumor repeated the more credible it becomes until eventually we believe it. This is nothing more than propaganda, and every level of our society practices it. But fortunately, the Camino offered us one of the greatest gifts—time—which allowed us to sort through the false and arrive at the truth of others' actions and intent.

I refused to talk to Yampah or have anything to do with him. As our journey continued over the next weeks, he shadowed us everywhere we stayed. He did many immature and inconsiderate things to get attention. He refused to shower so he smelled bad. He woke people up intentionally. Marjorie and Elaine were very nice to him, and he eventually was even mean to them. In Galicia, we encountered him walking very slowly and limping, as if he was in a trance, a study in misery both physical and mental. He growled at us, and Tannis spoke to him in a very comforting and soft way. The dramatic Dr. Jekyl and Mr. Hyde transformation that took place in front of our eyes eerily looked as if someone was changing from a monster to a human. We sensed that he was on the edge of having a breakdown. Later we met a young Spanish cyclist who was very upset as Yampah had just assaulted him on the trail for no reason. Whatever problems Yampah was carrying with him, his desire to be accepted and part of a group led him to try getting attention in any way he could. In the end, not one of us came home with a picture or a positive memory of him, and everyone remembered his name differently, if at all. Interestingly, all of his efforts to be seen resulted in his evaporating into thin air.

By the time we reached Reliegos, we were tired and hot. The last part of the day had proved especially difficult when we had walked so far. Tannis's knee ached, and I became very footsore. Our muscles were doing fine, but we had not anticipated the pressure on our feet and knees that built up as we walked day after day carrying the extra weight of our packs. We found our cute albergue in a converted school, with only seven other people staying there, for the fantastic price of four euros. Being in the more out of the way places and off the "twenty-miles-a-day tour book recommended stops" offered much more privacy.

We sat in the warm late afternoon sun and drew the bodegas at the edge of town. They were very fancy, featuring a variety of distinctive chimneys for air ventilation, iron grillwork, brick fronts, and red poppies growing on the top. One had a burgundy drape over the door, and one sported an iron gate. We enjoyed the relaxation, then continued it in the plaza. It was a perfect evening, warm enough for short-sleeved T-shirts late into the night. At the pilgrims' dinner we invited a lost looking young man to join us and share our meal. His name was Otto, and he was from Hungary. He had just lost his job, so he was hiking the Camino mostly for fun. His time was limited, so he was walking thirty-five to forty kilometers, about twenty-two to twenty-five miles, every day—about twice our normal distance. Ah, the power of youth!

Wine Bodegas

Reliegos to León
23,482 Steps, 10.0 Miles
April 26

Today I taught Tannis to beg. The French women began making noise at five forty-five and continued to get ready, creating much rustling and zipping action until six forty-five when they exited. We were thoroughly awake, so we gave up and got dressed, went downstairs to the showers, reorganized our packs, and finally entered the kitchen. The French women were still there eating breakfast. What had they been doing for two full hours? Exasperated, I looked in the cupboards and whimpered. The French women looked at me questioningly, and I sadly announced, "No café." They felt sorry for us and handed over instant coffee *and* sugar. All was forgiven, and Tannis was impressed by Begging Lesson Number 1. We gratefully scarfed down the coffee, along with some bread and about four ibuprofen each to ward off knee pain and foot swelling.

In the fabulous morning light, we walked a few kilometers to the next town where we had real café con leche and amazing cream-filled pastries. With sugar all over our faces, we smiled like the Cheshire Cat because they were so fantastically tasty. We had a chat with Luis, who referred to himself as the *abuelo loco*, or crazy grandfather. Luis was a Canadian, formerly from Mexico, with whom we had been walking on and off since early in the trip. We had not talked with him sooner because we assumed he was Spanish, and we were unaware that he spoke perfect English. He was feeling very sick and thought he might have had some bad water. He was in so much pain that I was going to give him some Aleve, but he told us he was on blood thinners due to his recent open-heart surgery. Yikes! I rapidly changed my mind about dispensing medication to him, and we became much more concerned about the seriousness of his discomfort. We were relieved when he decided to stop for the day. What an amazing feat to be walking the Camino with his health history and age.

After a few more kilometers, we reached the suburbs, complete with death-defying traffic on narrow roads without shoulders. Passing trucks practically sideswiped us off a bridge. We had to hold on and hug the rails to avoid a *tragicamente*. We decided it was time to take the bus, as advised in our guidebook, to avoid the heavy traffic, exhaust fumes, and hot cement on this dangerous stretch of road. Just as we were sweltering at the bus stop, Martien arrived in a taxi, leaning out the window and smiling at us! I was so glad to see him again, and all of the unfounded doubts that Yampah had planted vanished immediately. We hugged, laughed, and talked a million miles an hour catching each other up on our recent adventures, as we were transported into the center of Leon in a flash. Martien said, "I had been searching for you so hard. I finally decided that the only way to find you was just to let go, and ten minutes later, there you were!" Was it coincidence, fate, or faith that brought us back together? I could not believe we had made it all the way from Burgos to León in only seven days. Burgos felt as if it was still in the beginning part of the journey, and Leon seemed closer to the end. We had just *flown* across the meseta!

As soon as we found a nice little hostal in the center of León, Tannis received Begging Lesson Number 2. I asked the hostal owner for a hair dryer, and at first the answer was a definite no. I looked sad, pleaded that my hair was really bad, and looked thoroughly disappointed. Voila! Suddenly a hairdryer appeared, presumably belonging to his wife, by the terrified look on his face and his insistence that I return it the moment I had finished using it.

After lunch in a sunny sidewalk café, we visited the absolutely magnificent cathedral. Pointed Gothic arches surrounded the windows and led your eyes toward heaven. The soft golden stone was sculpted into lacy edges with the cerulean blue sky peeking through. What seem like hundreds of spires, formed like tall, thin vases, accented the steep rooflines and double-arched flying buttresses. Gargoyles and sculptures in the shape of evil little creatures peered down from the walls and peeked out from under arches. Once inside, the stained glass shone brilliant and magical, the rich and deep colors enveloping us in an intense, vibrant light.

The León cathedral, known as "The House of Light"

We walked around the outside of the cathedral and found a door that gave access to the upper areas of the building. The woman on duty said the last group had already gone up, and we had missed it. It was to be closed for the following two days, opening only after we would be gone from León. Begging Lesson Number 3 began as she informed us that it was impossible for us to join that last group. I really put everything I had into my request, taking her hands and theatrically getting down on my knees as I pleaded, "Oh please, please, *por favor*, señorita, we want to go up *so bad!*" In reality, I was not even sure what we were going to get access to, but it had to be good if it was off limits! She cracked a smile momentarily, then severely shooed a group of ten people out the door, firmly locking it behind them. She rolled her eyes, smiled widely, and pointed to the stairway up. Yippee! We followed her, scrambling up a series of scaffolding and ladders, un-nervingly labeled "Brio" like the toy building block sets. We scampered under the buttresses, which support the walls, and high walkways on ledges that disappeared with stairs spiraling up into round towers. We were convinced that this wondrous view of the structure was what there was to see and so very worth the pleading to get there. Just then the señorita put her fingers to her lips in a "quiet please" gesture and unlocked the door with a smile. We emerged into the top of the cathedral on a platform built directly under the main rose window. Infinitely luminous and brilliant light completely surrounded us, creating an ethereal experience. We could not believe that we got to stand right at the foot of a nearly one-thousand-year-old Gothic rose window, which had just had centuries of grime cleaned off it. We learned that the windows in the entire cathedral were being meticulously dismantled, cleaned, and reinstalled after being sandwiched between safety glass. The results were glorious. The León Cathedral is known as "The House of Light" and contains 19,400 square feet of some of the finest stained glass in the world. Some of the windows were nearly forty feet tall and dated as far back as the thirteenth century. We were so lucky to have had that once-in-a-lifetime experience and wondered how we are ever supposed to get what we want if we are not brave enough to ask for it. To make it absolutely perfect, the pipe organ began to play, filling the vaults with otherworldly music. Far below us, a bride walked down the aisle on the arm of her father, toward her God, her new husband, and her future.

We spent an equally exciting evening in the Plaza San Martien, a small square popular with the locals. Tiny pedestrian streets led into the plaza, which was crowded with sidewalk cafés and people out enjoying the warm night. We had a lovely dinner and wine as we watched several groups of bachelor and bachelorette parties parade through the town in costumes both unique and hilarious. One group of women all dressed in the white clothes with red scarf and sash typical of the Festival San Fermin, or "Running of the Bulls," with the bride dressed as a cow! A group of men all wore two-tone pink sweaters, while the groom wore the sweater *plus* a skirt, tights, and a wig. He had gorgeous legs, and I was very jealous. They were having so much fun. In the middle of all that frivolity, we heard a great deal of noise making, and then the Spanish president strolled through, talking with people and shaking hands. He walked right up to our table in that crowded little square, with no obvious security. What an incredible experience we had. León had outdone herself!

León
10,847 Steps, 4.62 Miles
April 27

We discovered how well the *roulades*, or metal curtains that pulled down over the windows and doors, really worked. They blocked out all of the light and sound, allowing us to sleep until eight thirty. Setting out for the day, we found that Martien had been out at the disco until four that morning so we left him sleeping. What a funny guy.

We wandered through beautiful León all morning. The original Roman walls and fortifications looked like red mud and rock rubble, but they have an amazingly thick and sturdy appearance. The Gardens of El Cid contained pieces of Roman aqueducts and antique pipes from the palace water system. Ornately carved capitals (tops) of pillars lay scattered at the foot of a lovely olive tree that looked to be very old.

We admired the house, now a bank that the famous architect Antonio Gaudi designed. Tame by Gaudi standards, still it immediately drew your attention because of its uniqueness. A wonderful sculpture of St. George, slaying a dragon with his sword, perched directly over the front door. We ambled along the parks skirting the river and bought straw hats at the open market before settling into a sidewalk café for lunch.

The Basilica of San Isidro is a Romanesque wonder built in the eleventh century over the much older Roman temple dedicated to the god Mercury. We did not want to interrupt mass, so we went to the museum where we wound our way up and down small spiral staircases to access the various sections. Gold, silver, ivory, gemstones, and inlaid wood in the form of casks, chalices, boxes, reliquaries, and processional crosses filled the treasure room. Everything was so ornate and beautifully crafted. How long must it have taken an artisan to complete each one of these masterpieces? The library contained huge illuminated songbooks similar to those we had seen at Yuso and Suso Monasteries. The library also contained hundreds of ancient regular-sized books. We take books and information for granted today, but how precious and priceless those must have been in the days before printing presses and widespread literacy. We completed the tour of San Isidro with a visit to the area holding the tombs where bright frescoes covered the walls and ceiling. Un restored, they displayed brilliant colors, even after nearly eight hundred years! Incredibly, they are still open to the air. They depicted scenes from the life of Jesus and also featured a series of agricultural motifs depicting farming activities for each month. The stone sarcophagi of many kings and queens, counts and children, rested peacefully around the vault.

Once again outside, we stood in the Puerta del Perdon, or door of pardon. It was the first of many that graced the Camino from there to Santiago. The heavy wooden door beneath the arch was locked, so you could not actually *pass through* it. However, we stood under it for some time and made a point to stand in every door of pardon all the way from León to Santiago. It is believed that if you were a sick or injured pilgrim, you could pass through the doorway and receive the same absolution of your sins as those who made it all the way to Santiago.

By making a pilgrimage to Santiago, tradition holds that a person is forgiven half of all the sins accumulated during his or her lifetime, and if the route is walked in a Holy Year, all of the sins are forgiven. The doors of pardon were established in harsher times when many pilgrims died or became too sick to continue their quest. Their creation must have been an affirmation that it was the intent to reach Santiago and the sacrifices made along the way that really counted.

As we were about to leave San Isidro, many bishops and church officials, decked out in fancy outfits, emerged from the mass. Soon several groups of police and military personnel arrived festooned in all their ribbons, decorations, and dress uniforms. A band strolled into sight, playing, followed by el presidente. We decided he had been following us! We walked right in behind him and listened to speeches in the cloister for fifteen minutes, enjoying the scene. There were children, tourists, and regular families all standing within a few feet of the president, unscreened, once more with no apparent security in evidence. There were no secret service people surrounding him, no limousines waiting to whisk him away, and no guns in sight. We felt very lucky once again.

We continued on to Hospital San Marcos, which was a pilgrims' hospice from the 1000s through the 1400s. The Knights of Santiago had their headquarters in the monastery for longer still. The current façade is a complicated mass of Renaissance motifs and stonework. More recently, it had been turned into a snazzy *parador* with a huge square in front. Paradors are historic buildings with architectural merit that have been lavishly restored and converted into very expensive, up-scale hotels. The Spanish government maintains and runs them in an effort to preserve cultural landmarks in a self-funding manner.

We sat on a bench and drew in the shade of the eighty-degree afternoon for several hours, having the long bench to ourselves. And then at about four thirty, or just post siesta, everything changed. An older woman asked politely if it would "molest me" if she sat down. I said, "Of course not," and took the hint to move my drawing materials, which were spread out all over the bench. Soon another lady came, then another, then another. Finally, they practically aced Tannis and me out

The quiet pleasures of a Spanish afternoon

of our bench, squinching us up at one end with our drawing materials on the ground. Obviously, we had taken *their* bench, and they wanted it back. Never mind that our entire view and perspective had changed after we had spent three hours drawing.

But in return for their seats, they gave us the pleasure of an entirely different scene. I am here to tell you that it was the greatest geriatric dating game that I had ever witnessed. All the ladies had dressed up in their fanciest, and had fixed up their hair to perfection. They had even buffed up their shoes and handbags. Taking their proper places on their bench, they talked to each other, pretending to ignore the old gentlemen who had begun to arrive. The men had prepared equally for the occasion, wearing suits, ties, and hats. Some had canes and wheelchairs, but such encumbrances did not prevent them from socializing and talking in the Sunday afternoon sunshine. It was quite a spectacle to witness, and so heartwarming. Their culture dictated that they look their very best and interact with others until the day they no longer can. The good news was that the parading and showing their best side to the opposite sex was not over until they hit the grave. With a smile and an adios, we left them to their quiet pleasures in their beautiful city of León.

León to Villar de Mazarife
22,546 Steps, 9.60 Miles
April 28

With Martien, we left beautiful León under sunny skies and taxied to the outskirts at Virgen del Camino. We were sad to move on after such a wonderful stay, but new adventures awaited us out there with new people and places to see. We split off the main road and immediately left civilization behind, walking through small villages on dirt and gravel roads. The soil on the small meseta changed to a rocky, red blanket covered with dried gray grasses and scrub brush. Alongside us, red poppies, statice, rockrose, and phlox lined the pathway. The scent of thyme, fennel, and lavender perfumed the air, while adding subtle color and texture to the landscape. Few houses dotted the landscape, and the sky opened wide before us. A mild breeze, temperature of about sixty degrees, and birds soaring overhead completed the scene to make a perfect day to resume walking.

We stopped in the tiny village of Oncina de la Valdoncina and ate oranges on a broken-down bench with our backs against a warm, earth-colored wall made of mud and stones. We petted and fed a small cream-colored burro that was tethered nearby. He was so fluffy and shaggy that you could hardly see his face beneath all the hair wildly emerging in all directions from his forehead. He had long fuzzy ears, big, soft eyes, and a most gentle disposition.

We arrived at our destination of Villar de Mazarife by one thirty. The old church across from our albergue, Tio Pepe, had a bell tower dominated by three huge stork nests. The storks were busily flying in and out, feeding their babies constantly. Crumbling in places, the tower looked as if it might tumble down under the weight of the giant nests.

Iron railings embellished with scallop shells surrounded the town's little plaza, and beautiful black iron lamps provided light. Small palm trees and olive trees bordered the square, and we enjoyed resting in the quiet peacefulness as the wind blew puffy white clouds across the sky. The day typified the timeless rhythm of the Camino: walking only as far as we felt like, stopping to pet the local animals, sharing juicy oranges in the sunshine with good friends, sitting quietly in the town square contemplating the storks, enjoying good food and drink for dinner, and getting a solid night's sleep with the anticipation of another gentle day on the horizon.

Villar de Mazarife to Hospital de Órbigo
25,359 Steps, 10.8 Miles
April 29

We took another easy, short day due to the pain in our feet and knees. Tannis was having some very intense pain, and we felt that we might be paying for the long days on the meseta. How odd, we thought, that

Storks nests in Villar de Mazarife

we now considered an eleven-mile day short. We have gotten stronger, lost weight, and reshaped our bodies over the miles of mountains, hills, mud, and weather. Getting up and just walking most of the day gave us a good feeling.

On this day, we had an easygoing route on small roads, over gentle hills, and through flat stretches. But all about us, activity buzzed. Busy and industrious farmers were working in their fields, plowing, raking, and planting. We passed many storks also busy in the fields, hunting for their hungry, growing families. And frogs serenaded us, singing incredibly loudly. They so impressed us with the volume and tone of their songs we laughed and wondered if they were in mating season.

We crossed the Río Órbigo on a fantastic, twenty-arched, medieval stone bridge built in the 1200s on the foundation of an old Roman Bridge. It is one of the longest bridges in Spain dating to the medieval era. At one time, the river must have run wide and treacherously to warrant a bridge so grand, but today "small stream" better described what flowed underneath.

Battles between the Visigoths and the Suevi took place in the area in 452, and King Alfonso III triumphed over the Moors in the late 800s. In 1434 it was the site of love spurned and honor restored. A lady had rejected Don Suero, and the young nobleman of Leon had placed an iron collar around his neck to symbolize that she still held him prisoner in love. He vowed not to let anyone pass over the bridge unless he declared his lady the fairest in the land. If the person refused, he challenged him to a joust. He declared he would break three hundred lances before he surrendered his vigil. Knights from all over Europe came to take up the challenge. Being a Holy Year, it was the height of pilgrimages and a great inconvenience for the numerous faithful following the route. Eventually 727 men took up his challenge before Don Suero broke the three hundred lances, after having wounded several and killed one, retiring undefeated and removing the iron collar. This tale of medieval romantic chivalry is thought to have inspired Cervantes's *Don Quixote*. Modern-day jousting tournaments are still held in the fields beside the bridge every summer.

After settling in our albergue, we went out to explore the town more thoroughly. Walking into the village across the bridge were Marjorie and Elaine! It was so wonderful finally to see them once more. We felt our family had come back together again after a long absence. The wind was beginning to blow very hard, and it felt as if winter had returned, so we went back to our snug albergue. It was hard to believe we were in Spain; it was nearly May, and it was so cold.

We drew in the courtyard and visited with our two friends, catching up on all of our adventures and laughing the afternoon away. Marjorie modeled a pair of big, square, wild, zebra-striped sunglasses, which she had purchased at a flea market. She posed and strutted like a runway model. What spirit and spunk she had! I felt compelled to draw her portrait right then and there. I portrayed her topless with the sunglasses and her bandana, catching her essence nicely. At least it looked like the person I saw inside of her: forever young, fun loving, proud, sassy, spirited, unafraid, unapologetic about who she was, and ready to take on the world. She delightfully proclaimed, "They are perky again!" That is what I want to be like when I am a seventy-five-year-old grandmother. She is my role model!

Hospital de Órbigo to Astorga
29,701 Steps, 12.65 Miles
April 30

We climbed steadily up all day through plowed fields, cattle farms, and interlocked hills. Trees have once again become part of the landscape, many scrub oaks and a few evergreens. All day we got closer to the tall mountains that we have been approaching from a distance for many days. I felt somewhat intimidated finally to be at the foot of those steep, snow-covered peaks.

We passed through a farm with black and white calves in a small enclosure. I called them, and they approached the fence. When I put my hand down to them, they sucked on my fingers as I scratched their heads. Tannis and Martien were appalled that I would stick my fingers

Marjorie

into the mouth of a large animal like that. But it was just like being at home on the ranch: they trust you and think they are going to get milk from your fingers as if they were nursing. They don't bite and are actually very gentle. We left them with a pat on the head and hoped they were not destined to be the veal at our next meal.

Soon after we left the calves, we came to a statue of a pilgrim about six feet tall. It wore the scarves, boots, hats, gloves, a walking staff, and all manner of discarded items from pilgrims' wardrobes. Some people had written messages and tucked them into the clothes. There was an entire grouping of rocks etched with figures and symbols, piles of pilgrim stones, and crosses. We stopped for a snack, and more closely examined what others had left behind.

We reached the pretty town of Astorga fairly early and set out to explore and draw in the square. Astorga was the ancient capital of the Astur tribe and later a full-blown Roman outpost, supporting the gold mines of the region. One can still see the walls, a forum, and all the things that went along with civilization at the time. In the Middle Ages it was an important Christian center with twenty pilgrims' hospitals serving the Camino.

In the square adjacent to the cathedral stood a building Antonio Gaudi designed as a bishop's palace in 1889. Inside, traditional rib vaulting carried a contemporary look. The ribs were made of red brick with white mortar, which gave them a striped candy-cane effect. Just above the bricks, bands of coral-colored, stylized patterns stood out against the white background of the ceiling vaults. The stained glass windows resembled 1920s art deco designs with draping and intertwining ribbons in pastel corals, greens, yellows, and blues.

Gaudi was always far ahead of his time. Born to a family of coppersmith artisans, he was exposed to design and rendering natural forms from an early age. He studied architecture in Barcelona for five years and received a degree in 1878 with the disclaimer, "Who knows if we have given this diploma to a madman or a genius? Time will tell." Indeed time did tell, and Gaudi's name became synonymous with the modernist movement. He is best known for the fantastic Sagrada Familia (Sacred Family) church in Barcelona, whose façade looks like melting

The bishop's palace designed in 1889 by Antonio Gaudi, Astorga

vegetation. Irregular lines and elements give the sense of a building in constant motion. The church incorporates eighteen towers into its huge, organically formed structure. The whole structure suggests the Gothic with an intuitive twist, resulting in an intricate fantasy. The bishop's palace here in Astorga gave a preview of his style that would later mature in the Sagrada Familia. In comparison, it looked tame, but the moment you saw it, you recognized its uniqueness—and likely the mastermind behind its design. Round towers with tall, sharply pointed roofs set off its sturdy design. Cloverleaf designs repeated in the windows, railings, and other architectural details. And the entryway had deeply flared, pointed vaults, which drew you in. The combination of massive stone blocks and rounded towers gave a feeling of lightness and solidity—as well as whimsy—all at the same time.

Tonight we scavenged through the cast-offs of fellow pilgrims. Tradition dictated that you could leave what you no longer wanted and others could take what they needed. We all found something we could not possibly live without, adding to the amazing variety of wardrobe combinations that form the pilgrim's fashion show. I found a *pink* hand towel with the name of a hotel in Paris on it. It perfectly suited me, the Perfumed Pilgrim who wears Chanel and maintains a girly persona. I was so thrilled that it became my towel for the rest of the journey. Marjorie and Elaine found a pink satin coverlet on one of the bunks that matched and brought it to me, tucking me into bed. Marjorie got a beer from somewhere. Martien found a new young woman to take out to dinner. Complete contentment settled upon all.

Astorga to Rabanal del Camino
29,249 Steps, 12.45 Miles
May 1

Marjorie could not walk this morning so she took a taxi, along with all of our backpacks, to Rabanal. What a sense of freedom we experienced walking without the packs. We all felt the relief in our knees and feet, and it was like a holiday. I felt as if I was flying. Elaine and Martien both walked with us, and we enjoyed it so much. Times of laughter as well as moments of companionable silence held us together as we walked through the morning so cold and clear you could see your breath in steamy puffs.

The landscape was changing and, with it, the materials used for the buildings. Clay houses gave way to stone structures, and red tile roofs to slate or thatched roofs. Stone walls lined the fields. And pine forests were beginning to appear, climbing the mountainsides. Flocks of woolly sheep grazed and milled around us on the trails. We climbed steadily through scrubland and oak trees toward the mountains. The earth was deep red, and the path we were following was a golden raw sienna. The pink heather grew five feet tall, and violet colored wild flowers carpeted broad sections. Hiding among the flowers were iridescent, multi-colored lizards nearly a foot long.

We stopped at the tiny village of Santa Catalina de Somoza and ate our picnic lunch on a stone bench in the sunshine of the church portal. Tannis said that her dreaming was increasing and becoming more vivid as our time on the Camino increased. The comfort of the solitude had left her experiencing times of no thoughts, just peacefulness. Full of gratitude for these healing times, she had been feeling less brittle and shattered than when we began the journey. Her dreams of her parents allowed her to think of them in happier times without their death masks. The Camino seemed to have taken on its own life, pulling and easing us along to Santiago.

We entered the town of Rabanal del Camino where the stone streets were inset with river rocks in patterns. We had since left the storks and their nests far behind. And here, the stones in the buildings ranged from golden, yellow ochre to rich iron red.

The Gaucelmo Confraternity ran this lovely albergue in a beautifully restored building. The volunteers Hilary and Orlando met on the Camino, fell in love, and never returned to their normal lives. They were so gracious and kind, embodying the spirit and the magic of the Camino. Having seen his share of pilgrims passing through, Orlando felt that many people traveling the Camino lacked the proper mental and physical preparation, and for that he felt regret. The albergue had

Stone fences and sheep lead us back into the mountains near Rabanal del Camino

a beautiful garden and a small library with a wonderful warm fire. The chimney made a whistling sound, but I was warm for the first time in quite a long while and settled into a deep sense of contentment.

As I sat by the fire, a handsome, blond young German man around thirty years old came in and sat down, looking at me guiltily. We had registered at an albergue a few days ago and had sensed some mildly anti-American feelings from him. We checked out of the albergue and registered at a different one, and for several days we kept running into him. He would study us sheepishly until we began to engage him in light conversations at each encounter. Tonight, just to be nice, I asked him his name. He said, "Atilla." **NO WAY!** I was biting my tongue in an admirable yet excruciating manner when Tannis blurted out, "As in Atilla the Hun?" He said very seriously, "Yah, yah, it has been cause for laughter all my life." Unable to stand it any longer, we both burst out laughing. Recovering herself, Tannis said, "We are laughing with you, not at you." This was so blatantly and obviously untrue that all three of us broke down in giggles. I mean, for crying out loud, what had his parents been thinking? With a name like Atilla the Hun, no wonder the poor guy had a chip on his shoulder the size of Germany and wanted to rape and pillage everything in his path. We were actually pretty lucky to have escaped with only a few "Microsoft sucks" type comments. We were wracking our brains trying to think of a nickname, but "Tilla," "Atty," or "Hun" seemed somewhat inappropriate and provocative. I guess it had to be a straight-faced, "Hey, Atilla, how's it hanging?" or nothing. Of course that would be totally impossible to say. However, the whole conversation broke the ice, and I told him that I was sure he was a very nice young man, but we had just started off on the wrong foot. We just began calling him "Atilla," and eventually we all stopped giggling every time we said it. He became a fun member of our group, I believe slowing down to our pace so that he could keep company with Marjorie, Elaine, Martien, and us. So went life, and laughs, on the Camino.

Rabanal del Camino to Acebo
28,800 Steps, 12.27 Miles
May 2

Last night Martien gave Marjorie and Tannis "treatments" on their knees. He said he had learned the technique from his mother. He just put his hands on the area that was afflicted and asked God to heal it. The room was very quiet and still, and he asked that they receive the energy, talking in a quiet, soothing way. Marjorie said her knee was beginning to feel better with each treatment, and Tannis reported an energy like a blue light or laser going straight to her knee. Incredibly, her pain was much diminished on our hike through the mountains in the following days.

We put Marjorie on the taxi along with our packs and set off up the mountain. By putting our packs on the taxi and splitting the fee, we all could afford the luxury of walking pack-less. The arrangement also let Marjorie know that in addition to taking care of herself she was helping us by taking the load off our knees and feet for a few days in an effort to avoid permanent injuries that might have stopped us from finishing the Camino. We had pushed our bodies as far as they would go without a mutiny or a relief from the burdens on our backs. I felt as if the arches of my feet were literally ready to rip out, not to mention my Achilles tendon ready to burst with the swelling and irritation. Knowing our packs will be safely at the next albergue with Marjorie, although we miss her company on the trail, gives us all renewed energy.

Huge pink heather, ivory and yellow Scotch broom, and naked trees silhouetted against the blue sky surrounded us. The grasses in the high alpine meadows shimmered in the gentle waves of wind. Herds of soft brown milk cows with their calves lounged contentedly in the grass and wildflowers. We climbed steadily to pine forests as we came eye to eye with the mountaintops we had been dreading. All that intimidation and dread, yet by just putting one foot in front of the other and pressing on, we had done it! We had conquered the highest point on the entire Camino and felt justly proud. We had learned what we could

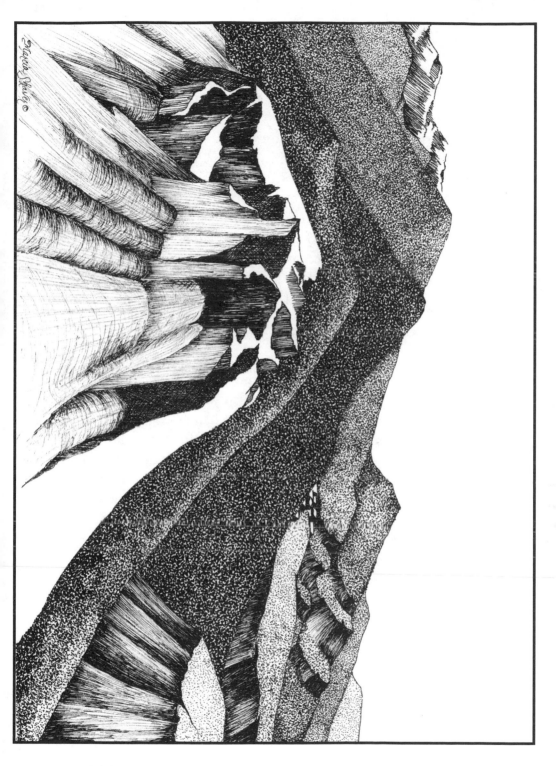

The highest point on the Camino near the village of Acebo

accomplish with determination, and we would never have to be afraid of those mountains again.

The most incredible part of the day was being at the top of the mountains at the Cruz de Ferro, or Iron Cross. What began as a pagan custom of leaving stones to mark the high passes was Christianized by the addition of the simple iron cross on a tall, weathered, wooden pole. For pilgrims of all nations it is one of the simpler yet personally important symbols of the Way of St. James. Elaine, Tannis, and I stood in silent contemplation, linked arm in arm, as a group of Germans sang a hauntingly beautiful song in the pine-scented air. Elaine said quietly, "With all the love in my heart." I felt we merged the power and love within us, and then we added our stones to the towering pile at the base of the cross along with our thoughts and prayers for each one. As Tannis added a stone for her dad, the tears began to stream down her face, and she felt his presence very strongly there with her. I added stones—for a friend recovering from cancer, then for my husband in the hopes he could get out of his stressful job and have a happier existence, and for Justin, son of my body and heart of my heart, that he might be more well. I threw a stone onto the pile for myself, and it came back to me! Perhaps I was not yet ready to let some things go. Or did I no longer need to let anything go, as I had already done it? Did the stone return to me symbolic of a journey that had come full circle?

Next I tossed a stone onto the pile for a person who had been very viscous and mean to our family over the years. The strangest thing happened. On the mountaintop, all of the anger and resentment I had felt about her scattered with the wind, silently drifting away with the birds soaring overhead. She dissipated into nothingness, an anonymous being. I felt profoundly sorry for that person. I thought, "People like that are not happy, and they have nothing. If she believes all of the things she said about us, then she never knew us. She never knew one of the finest men she would ever meet, my husband, and that is her loss. And if she doesn't believe all the things she said about us, then she must be wracked with guilt." I simply felt at peace, knowing what was true, what my values and ethics were, and who I was. It was an intense moment, a celebration of letting go the hurt and anger while recognizing all of the good blessing my life. It was a release and a new beginning.

We all cried and were surprised by the powerfully emotional component to the symbolic act. We walked in silence for about twenty minutes, then paused for a picnic in the sunshine at a lovely meadow.

After cresting the mountains, we walked steadily downward. We came to Manjarín, which merely amounted to a bend in the road with a hippie albergue. It was a real sixties' flashback! Many people had stopped there, and a festive air of celebration pervaded the scene. Perhaps those travelers needed an emotional release after their experiences at the Cruz de Ferro. But we continued downward on very steep, rocky pathways until we reached El Acebo, a small village with stone houses and slate roofs. The one main, narrow street wound steeply toward the valley below. Exterior stone steps on the homes led to wooden balconies and created a completely charming scene. We sat in the sun on a hillside at the top of town and drew the mountains that we had been traversing. They formed many layers of soft blue silhouettes, which gradually receded into the distance.

After drawing, we joined Martien, Elaine, Marjorie, Atilla, and several new friends in the town square and shared a bottle of wine and local snacks in the sunshine. It was warm and beautiful at the top of the world. Everyone seemed so happy and relaxed, smiling and sharing stories. I wondered if the subdued tone had resulted from everyone resolving personal issues at the Cruz de Ferro or from the slower process of walking so far and releasing tensions a little at a time. Perhaps it was a combination of both. Snacks inevitably turned into a fantastic dinner at the albergue, and we went to bed tired but full of smiles and peacefulness.

Acebo to Ponferrada
32,627 Steps, 13.9 Miles
May 3

We once again loaded our packs on a taxi with Marjorie and Elaine, who felt the steep downhill trek all day would be a disaster on their knees. Freedom from our packs! We set off in the sunshine to an absolute wonderland of nature. We traveled down rocky paths through gorges and open hills covered in intense purple Spanish lavender, ivory and yellow iridescent broom, red and orange poppies, salvias and various pink and violet wildflowers. Birds sang and large, bare, twisted trees added a graphic linear element to all of the soft colors. The fragrance of lavender and broom permeated the air. Rocks jutted out of the carpet of colors, covered in delicately painted pink, green, and yellow succulents. We had five miles of pure magic and then emerged from the countryside at a lovely medieval bridge and entered the village of Molinaseca. Its picturesque narrow street provided a perfect place to pause, savor a café con leche, and think about the magnificent landscape we had just traveled through.

The remaining miles into Ponferrada kept along main roads and through suburban approaches to the city. We reached the albergue and were greeted by Marjorie, Elaine, and Atilla having a beer in the sunny courtyard. Marjorie had scored a semi-private room for us four women and delivered our packs to our bunks. What a welcome luxury that was! We restored our spirits with a shower and an hour of companionship in the warm spring afternoon before going into town to explore.

The Knights Templar Fortification, which once protected pilgrims from bandits, was an amazing structure complete with turrets, arrow-slit windows, crenellated battlements, and huge round towers. It loomed over the Río Sil and valley stretching westward. This fairy tale castle flew brightly colored flags above the entrance gate, reached by crossing a bridge and navigating the raised iron grill, which could be slammed shut to discourage attackers. Excavations have shown that the site was originally a Celtic settlement, and through the centuries,

Knights Templar castle, Ponferrada

it was a fortification held by the Romans, Visigoths, Muslims, and the Christians. The ruins of the Roman fort were donated to the Knights Templar in 1178, and they began the construction of the castle in 1218, taking sixty-four years to complete. But they occupied it for only twenty years as the Vatican dissolved the Order of the Knights Templar in 1312. In the centuries following, it changed hands many times and served many functions. Its enormous size (96 by 164 meters, or approximately 16,000 square meters) allowed it to function simultaneously as a fort, palace, monastery, and a miniature city. Self-contained, it featured a plaza, reception hall, chapel, chapter house, cemetery, stables, sleeping quarters, kitchens and dining areas, hospitality suites for invited guests, and dungeons for less desirable visitors. We felt the presence of all those who made up the community as we wandered along the castle walls and peered through narrow tower windows. Coats of arms and the Templar motto can still be seen carved on the walls. Translated from Latin it stated, "If the Lord does not protect the city, those who guard it guard in vain."

We found Martien and our new pilgrim friends Reinhardt and Yoakhim in the plaza having a beer and happily yakking away in German. Martien was a bundle of frantic energy in his nicotine-deprived state since he had quit smoking at the Cruz de Ferro yesterday. As we shared dinner in a sidewalk café, we learned Reinhardt's story as Martien translated. Reinhardt had suffered an injury, which resulted in his inability to walk fully. He suffered for several years before having a surgery that corrected his nerve damage and restored him to good health. Accompanied by his friend Yoakhim, he was walking to Santiago to give thanks to God for the miracle he felt in his recovery. The kind, soft-spoken, gentle giant of a man felt his obligation to God very keenly, and his sincerity and humility touched my heart.

Ponferrada to Villafranca Del Bierzo
34,148 Steps, 14.55 Miles
May 4

Good news! Atilla has proposed marriage to Marjorie in exchange for a Canadian green card! She is thrilled and accepted immediately. How clever of her to snag a hunky thirty-year-old from another continent! We feel that we should warn Atilla that Marjorie probably had three lifetimes of inappropriate fun before he was even born. However, we refrained from telling him because we did not want to jinx the whole proposal as we all want to be bridesmaids. This morning Tannis said, "Congratulations on the blessed event." Atilla asked, "Vhere is my bride?" We told him she was in the kitchen cooking his breakfast. He replied that was good; it was just where he wanted her to be. Uh-oh, I smelled a marital dispute in the making! In the mean time, we continued to ponder over the question; "Will we have to call her Marjorie the Hun?"

After loading our packs and Marjorie on to a taxi, Elaine, Tannis, and I set off through town. Martien was far ahead, not really walking with us, but it was comforting to know he would be our companion for the evening. I thoroughly enjoyed Elaine's company and her solid, sensible approach to life. We laughed at all the small things and smiled our way through the tiny mountain towns along the way. In one such village, we stopped at a vending machine for water. We realized with fascination that the center section of the machine featured all sorts of products for the hot Spanish nights. A wide selection ranged from the standard condoms to some mysterious devices used for enhancing the moment. One of us did not know what they were for, and by the time we finished enlightening her, we were laughing so hard we were doubled over on the pavement. Two Spanish men had paused in their daily routines to stare at us, so Elaine flashed them a hand signal which meant OK to us, but in some cultures meant "You asshole." Way to offend a whole continent! By then Elaine and Tannis both were blushing furiously, but I was thinking, "What an awesome vending machine. If the Pringles and chocolate do not get you off, you have other choices. *Emergencia on the calle mayor!* Tragicamente if we can't get our hot sex toys right now!" Well, it did make sense, as the stores were always closed so one really could not plan ahead. Oh I got it … *that* is what the siesta is really for. We agreed that we must inform Marjorie and Atilla at the first opportunity.

We passed through many vineyards clinging to the hillsides. The vines were just beginning to leaf out, and the patterns of the planted rows made our way very beautiful. Loading the branches of the cherry trees, bountiful small, formed fruit foreshadowed a good harvest. Topping the houses, gray slate roofs provided a contrast to the bright yellow-green fields sprinkled with thousands of thriving red poppies. In the very warm, summer-like temperatures, the roses were blooming and full of sweet perfume. Rhododendrons and many of the plants that we have in Western Washington filled the countryside, reminding me of home, and signaled our entry into a new region of higher rainfall and more moderate temperatures than found in the interior lands.

Where the rivers Valcarce and Burbia converged, forming the west end of the fertile basin, sat Villafranca, an interesting town perched strategically in the mountains. Situated at the beginning of the narrow valley leading to the Cebreiro Pass, it has been inhabited since antiquity but became a major pilgrimage stop early in the twelfth century. By the mid twelfth century, half of the inhabitants were foreign, thus the name Villafranca, meaning "foreign town." In our exploration of the town, we came upon a spectacular, huge wisteria with a trunk the size of a tree. The limbs stretched far in every direction, laden with fragrant purple clusters of blossoms. Our curiosity got the better of us, and we inquired at the bar where the locals proudly informed us that it is the biggest and oldest wisteria in all of Spain, over 250 years old. It was growing when America was in its infancy and still a British Colony. Yet in this very spot, lovingly tended as history moved across the landscape and time marched on, this beautiful plant lived and grew. What an incredible thought.

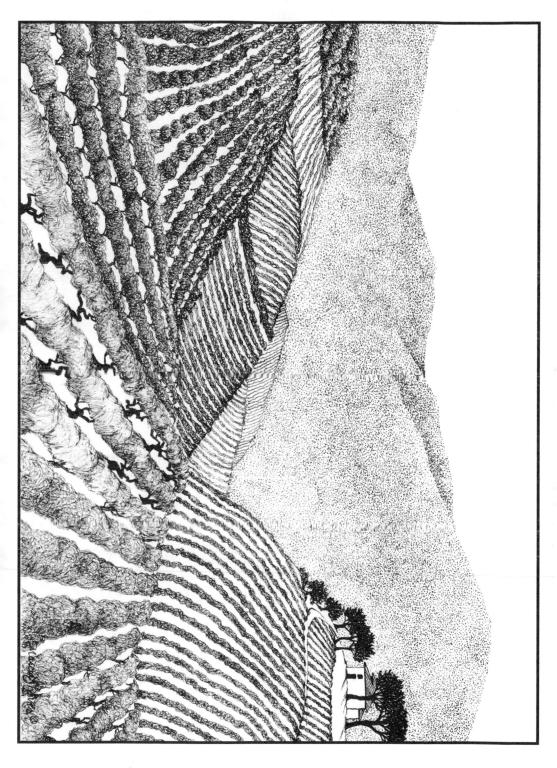

Vineyards in the mountainous region approaching Villafranca

Villafranca Del Bierzo to Las Herrerías
35,028 Steps, 14.92 Miles
May 5

Marjorie and Elaine departed by taxi this morning to jump ahead sixty miles through the mountains. They felt that if they were to finish the Camino, they needed to get past the steepest mountains due to the knee injuries they were suffering. Everyone's Camino journey differs, and they made a wise and cautious decision. I felt sad that we would probably not catch up with them again and that this might be the last time we would see them. However, their departure provided a good time to reflect on what putting our packs on the taxi had meant for us. Our knees and feet had highly benefited from the rest for a few days. But on the down side, we had felt tied to a schedule, which ran counter to the simplicity of the Camino. With our packs waiting for us at a predetermined location, we had to go to a certain destination whether we were tired or not. Sometimes, we passed right through some lovely villages without the luxury of stopping to explore them. And, traveling without my pack began to make me feel weak. I had been feeling very strong and had welcomed the timelessness in just getting up, putting on my pack, and walking through the country. Yes, we had had a goal each day, but we had left it fluid, open to change, and had not depended on anyone or anything else. We had remained self-contained and self-sufficient. The section of country we were now hiking was one of the most difficult and also one of the most beautiful. We had absolutely no reason to rush, as we were a couple of days ahead of our schedule. I decided that I did not want to take taxis, but I also did not want to arrive so exhausted that I could not enjoy the way. We did not need to share in the frenzy of the pace of others rather than enjoying where we were. Keeping to the schedules of others was destroying the rhythm of the Camino for us. We longed to return to the slower pace of walking, which allowed more contemplative time, writing, and drawing. Feebly, we refrained from just saying "no" when we felt that the destination was too far because we valued the company of our new friends. In the spirit of livestock being herded to market, we began to chant, "This little piggy went to market, this little piggy stayed home …" We ended with an appropriate little piggy squeal, "Weak, weak, weak, weak!"

We had previously committed to put our packs on a taxi and walk as far as Las Herrerías with Martien. When he arrived, we realized the only taxi in town had taken Marjorie and Elaine 120 kilometers away and might not return for hours. In keeping with our earlier resolution, we discussed whether just to carry our packs today or not. The regular route followed a paved road under a freeway, so we had chosen the optional pathway to Pradela over a very steep and difficult pass due to its reported beauty. We felt that to walk the high route while carrying our packs that day might be unwise, as we might inflame the injuries that we had just spent four days trying to heal. We sighed and walked to the next albergue where we met Alberto, the crazy Brazilian who transported *mochilas* (backpacks) for pilgrims. He said, "No problem, I deliver bags to Herrerías!" Skeptically I peered into the back of his van, which was already stuffed to the ceiling with packs headed somewhere else. He declared flamboyantly, "Don't worry! I mark them!" He proceeded to slap a two-inch-long piece of tape on them, discovered his pen would not write, and threw his arms around us. "No problem! Marked! I remember! Come have café with me now. Ha ha ha!" Was this a happy laugh or the fiendish cackle of a mochila-molesting, half-dressed, wild-haired guy from the jungles of Brazil, who I could not guarantee understood English? Even though I was sure I would never see my pack again, I was desperate for coffee so I agreed. Not that I cared because I had a love/hate relationship with my pack, but it did contain my Chanel #5 and my pink towel. Some things seem exceedingly important when you suddenly have no control over your life.

After sucking down a café grande, we said adios to Alberto and our bags, potentially forever. We relinquished control and followed the yellow arrows to town, praying for another Camino miracle. Three different routes led to our destination, and Martien wanted to take the hardest one. We had read our guidebook and determined that it was not well marked and crossed three mountains, so Tannis and I opted for the middle route. This still took a much higher and more difficult route than along the road, but it was more scenic and we had less chance of getting lost. We told Martien he better get going if he was going to walk the high, wild, less-traveled route alone. We gave him a hug and told him that it was just in case he got lost and we never saw him again. He looked alarmed. He said to send a helicopter out looking for him if he did not show up. We nonchalantly said, "Well, yes, but first we have to have dinner at ocho media (eight thirty). Then we would have at least one bottle of wine, and by the time it gets dark about ten we will ask '*Dónde está Martien?*' (Where is Martien?) It could be like a giant game of Where's Waldo. We could probably trace you and your red fleece jacket on Google Earth." He immediately declared, "You beetches!"We sent him on his way, frowning in a concerned way. He went about ten steps, then circled back several times boomerang style, consulting his compass. Meanwhile, we were still in the town square. Finally he motored off, and we took our time going to the bank machine, then shopped for a fabulous pair of chic sunglasses for Tannis costing only five euros. I played with a kitten. A nun and I helped free it from a collar it was caught up in. We went to a bar and hit the *servicios,* or restrooms. We took pictures and circumnavigated a large church. When we finally crossed the river, we ran into Martien still going in circles. By then it was eleven, and we had not yet left Villafranca. Martien stalked up in frustration and declared, "I go wiff you! I have been looking for dis focking road for an hour!" We assured him that he had made the right decision as it would actually be very bad to go by yourself on a trail that was not well marked and very difficult if you could not even find your way out of town.

We started up the steep Calle Pradela, as instructed in our guide-book, and no fewer than six Spanish people helpfully directed us the other way. One lady was even hanging out of her window waving at us frantically, and there were signs posted warning that you must be exceedingly fit to attempt the route. Undeterred, we headed **straight up** to dismayed looks that spoke volumes, "You will never make it. Don't say I did not try to warn you." Ha! The nearly vertical climb to the mountaintop in the heat of the day was so worth it and landed us in heaven on earth. If God taught landscaping to master gardeners, we had found his heavenly classroom. The pink heather, yellow and ivory broom, cream and yellow rockroses, purple Spanish lavender, pink and white wildflowers all cascaded down the hillsides and draped over the narrow stony trail. In the distance, the blue mountains receded steeply, revealing the passes we had crossed. Far below us, the river rushed, and other pilgrims looked like ants along the road. We were walking on the top of the world, serene and fantastically colorful. Except for two other hikers, we had the route to ourselves. Pine forests, fresh and sweet smelling, cloaked the summit, and we carried the scent with us as we wound back down to the valley floor through groves of huge old chestnut trees, feeling lucky to have had a truly magical experience.

After rejoining the main route at Trabadelo, we walked for several miles on a secondary road under the freeway. That part was not so nice, but it made our welcome at Las Herrerías even sweeter. Alberto was true to his word, and our packs were waiting for us as promised in our immaculately clean room. Our little hotel sat on a river with cows pastured right under the balcony where we were drawing. The grass was so thick and tall that it half buried the cows. Stone walls and fruit trees separated the pastures. The temperature was perfect, and the trees shimmered in the evening light. The mountains that we were to cross the next day formed a backdrop of soft pink, cloaked in miles of heather. A bare, intricately branched tree framed the softer fields. The landscape presented a collection of contrasting colors and textures, forming a complex yet soothing scene, and contentedly, we sat in wooden rocking chairs on the balcony until twilight drew near.

The handsome proprietor cooked us a fabulous dinner. We feel like royalty with the white linen tablecloths, crystal stemware, and cobalt blue dishes. The rock walls and open beamed ceilings lent a simple yet elegant touch to the quiet restaurant. As if that was not enough, Tannis gave me a foot massage before bed. I had found paradise!

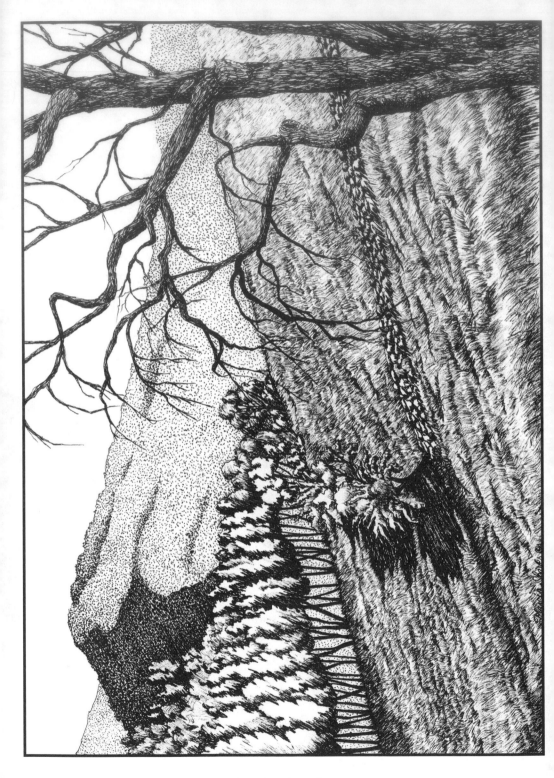

Lush meadow lands at las Herrerías

Las Herrerías to O'Cebreiro
18,066 Steps, 7.70 Miles
May 6

We slept quietly and luxuriously until seven thirty. The smell of clean, crisp sheets is something I will never take for granted again. After a leisurely breakfast, we put our mochilas on a taxi for the last time. We insisted that they go only as far as the top of the mountain at O'Cebreiro so that we could ultimately determine how far we would walk.

The valley sat quietly at the bottom of very steep mountains. The river's melody and the singing of birds, overlaid by the quiet stirring of cows and chickens, presented the only sounds as we left paradise. We crossed the river on a fifteenth-century bridge and began our steep climb toward La Faba on a small paved road. The views grew increasingly spectacular as we climbed and began our final assault on the mountains toward O'Cebreiro. Although we had passed the highest point on the Camino a few days ago, we continued our steep up and down journey each day. In the brilliant sunshine, you could see for miles in every direction. We walked along lanes with stone fences covered in ferns and moss, bordering steep, verdant pastures. Happy, soft brown milk cows concentrated on sunbathing and eating all day while dogs lay watchfully near. It was an idyllic setting and lovely to walk through, a land of simple hand farming as it has been done for centuries. (Of course, we encountered the occasional John Deere tractor as well.) The hills across the valley were pink with heather and heath. We felt so lucky to see this breathtaking, serene region on a clear day, as the normal weather tended toward fog, rain, and even snow in the summer.

When we reached the marker signaling that we had crossed into Galicia, we had tears in our eyes. Suddenly we felt so emotional we could not speak. I thought, "We have arrived in the last province of Spain. Here we are nearly to Santiago! I can hardly believe it. We have walked hundreds of miles over mountains and plains, through hailstorms and sixty-miles-per-hour winds, under lightning and thunder. We have had blisters, swollen feet, sore knees, saddle sores, heavy packs, and mud slicks. But we have also found great food and wine, sunshine, fields of wildflowers and stone fences, plains of wheat stretching as far as the eye can see, fabulous and interesting people. Yet, here we are, just Tannis and I. We have walked across most of an entire country, a distance equal to walking from Seattle to Helena, Montana! This moment has always been so remote and so far in the future that it seemed impossible we would ever get this far. Yet, here we are. One step, and then another, and then the one more that we did not think we could take. I am so proud of us, and so in awe that we have come so far. These fifty-plus women's bodies have put one boot in front of the other, and now we are close to our goal." What an incredibly beautiful feeling it was, heightened on such a beautiful day.

We reached the top of the world at O'Cebreiro around one o'clock. We saw Martien briefly before he forged on for another eight kilometers. We tried to tell him that we might not see him again as we were thinking of taking a short day. However, he was so sure we would follow him that we barely said good-bye. We had bocadillas and freshly squeezed orange juice, then decided we had no reason to rush away from such a magical village. In this, the land of Galicia, O'Cebreiro had some of the oldest remaining buildings on the Camino, some built in the 900s. It is said that the Holy Grail, used at the Last Supper by Christ himself, was hidden here during the Middle Ages. Near the church is a statue of Elias Valiña, a modern-day miracle worker. A local priest, he inspired and worked toward the revival of the Camino in the 1960s and 1970s. Without his writing, his personal dedication, and his hard work, the Camino probably would not exist as it does today: alive and well, with an energy and vitality that grows with each year. It is a testament to how one person can make a difference in this world and touch so many lives.

The local gray stone offered handsome material for the sturdy, slate-roofed houses, which intermixed with round rock houses, called *pallozas*. Thatched conical roofs made from the local dried broom topped them off and had ropes of braided broom at the top to hold the thatch in place. They had no chimneys; the hearth fire was placed in the center of the dwelling. Traditionally, meats were hung in the top of

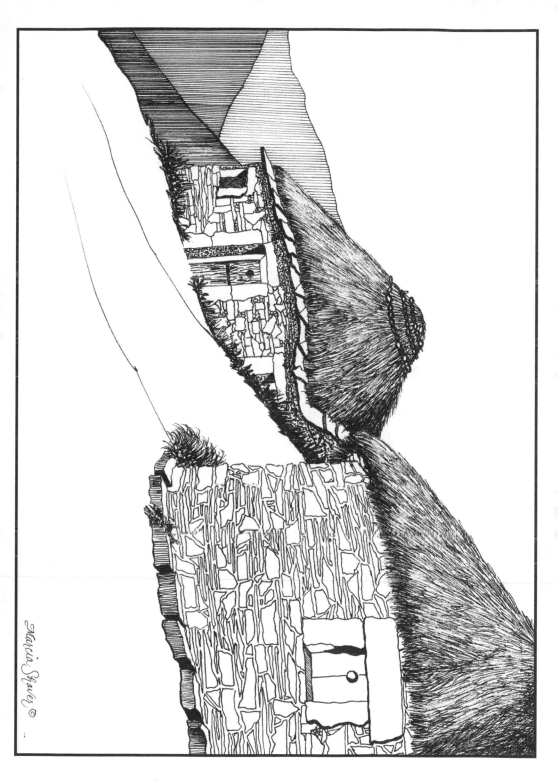

Thatched roof "pallozas" at O'Cebreiro

the roof and became cured as the smoke escaped through the thatch. They appeared to grow organically from the steep hillsides, sometimes only one or two feet tall on the uphill side. They were typical of the old style of traditional Celtic buildings. What character they had!

O'Cebreiro to Triacastela
32,858 Steps, 14.0 Miles
May 7

By seven forty, we were walking through the beautiful, clear morning. We had entered a land of stone fences and lush pastures, a perfect dairy farming region. It felt good to be back among all the animals again. As we were walking down one of the lanes, a herd of cows came out of a stone corral toward us. I told Tannis just to stand right behind me and be very still. The cows flowed calmly around us like a river, their sides brushing us, the heat rising off their bodies.

Up and down we climbed over several mountains and wound our way through tiny farming hamlets. Many of the small, picturesque towns consisted of only a few stone houses, interspersed with barns. They clustered very close together, linked by a road that was more like a footpath. In one tiny village, an old señora emerged from her house to offer us fresh, hot crepes sprinkled with sugar. They melted in our mouths and filled the air with enticing aromas. They whetted our appetite and made us hungry, so we paused in the next village for bocadillas on a stone bench. Two German shepherd puppies cavorted in the sunshine and played with us as we ate.

We reached Triacastela, meaning "three castles," in a rainstorm. None of the castles still existed, but the lovely town sat in a pretty valley. Founded in the 800s, Triacastela was historically important for near this city lay the quarry from which the limestone for the cathedral at Santiago was taken. In the twelfth century, pilgrims carried the stones from here all the way to the kilns at Casteñeda, one hundred kilometers away. The stone blocks were then finished and transported on to Santiago to become the magnificent cathedral.

As the rain lashed the windows and the storm clouds swirled, we sat comfortably on a top bunk bed in our albergue, drawing the scene before us. The mountains rose abruptly from the valley floor, dominating the view and cradling the stone church of the town. Influenced by the medieval history of the area, I saw its roof covered in dragon scales. Made of local dark gray slate and roughly hewn into random-shaped shingles, the overlapping slates interlocked at the ridgeline like arrowheads protruding in opposite directions. The different tones of gray stone and steep mountains, combined with the cold rainstorm made us feel as if we were in a northern European village.

We cooked a pasta dinner and stayed in our cozy albergue. As I was sautéing the vegetables, two young Spanish men came in, inhaled deeply, threw their arms wide and proclaimed, "Mama!" We laughed, and they joined us for pasta and a glass of wine. I loved the comfortable, multi-generational mingling that occurred in Spain. In America those young men, about the age of our children, would probably not have given us the time of day, let alone sat down for a conversation. Then again, I *was* cooking dinner.

Later, we met a Japanese boy, who had just graduated from high school, and his father. He told us that he did not get accepted into university so he was walking the Camino with his dad. His actions so impressed me because their culture viewed being rejected from university as a huge disgrace, like a stamp of failure for life. Yet, his father had taken time off work to walk the Camino with him rather than be disappointed. The father is so gentle with the son. We talked for a long while, and I was convinced that the skills the young man possessed would lead him to a full and rewarding life. He was sincere, vulnerable, honest, full of enthusiasm, creative, physically fit, and mentally acute. I believe he was a musician as well. He interacted across the cultures and generations beautifully, as well as spoke fairly fluent English. His self-confidence and sense of adventure burned brightly, enveloping us all. We would likely not see them again as they were covering many more miles each day than we at our relaxed pace.

The terrain had challenged us physically, but tranquility and calmness had surrounded us during our travel. Tannis had the beginning

Slate roofs and steep mountains define the town of Triacastela

of a cold and felt a bit tired. We had felt the added strain with the pack on again, but in many ways, it had also felt good. It was good to be self-contained and have everything we needed right there with us. We made our own schedule and stopped or continued as we wished. It was life on a basic level and gave a sense of freedom quite unlike anything else. The Camino was indeed a special experience. I decided that it was like a giant summer camp for adults. Someone cooked all your meals, which became very similar. You slept with thirty to fifty people each night in bunk beds in a room filled with snores and other noises which I will not elaborate on. You met and played with all kinds of interesting people from all over the world. You went outdoors and did sports every day and came in exhausted. You chose activities to fill the quiet times with writing, personal meditation, or art assignments.

Of course, we went beyond normal summer camp activities, walking until we dropped. At the end of each day, we fell with utter exhaustion into bed and dreamt of doing it all again the next day. I suspected that when we returned home, we would look back on the whole experience as one of the best times of our life. All adults should get to go to summer camp and come home refreshed, with a totally new perspective. For that matter, all the world's leaders should be required to go on the Camino together. With their only possessions in a pack on their back, they should stay on the Camino until they have bonded sufficiently to get along together and lay the foundation for a more peaceful world.

Triacastela to Samos to Aguiada
30,878 Steps, 13.15 Miles
May 8

The warm and humid air felt soft to our skin because of all the moisture it contained. We followed a river with high cliffs surrounding us, leaving the road at San Cristobal and continuing on intimate country lanes that snaked across the landscape. Moss and ivy, green and spongy looking, draped the trees. Fences made of slate, nearly five feet tall,

Slate fences of Galicia

stood straight up. Held together by only a small wire, the organic shapes undulated along the contours of the earth. Small creeks ran through the villages and fields, lined in Queen Anne's lace and cobalt blue wild flowers similar to forget-me-nots. The farmers of Galicia do not use herbicides or pesticides, so all of the fields were lush and green with a profuse riot of colorful wildflowers and native plants.

The tiny hamlets linked the beautiful farmland like a string of beads and continued the rolling pathways onto their very narrow streets with stack-stone walls of the local rocks. Wonderful, small, neat vegetable gardens, newly planted, were just starting to grow. In this farming community, many of the slate-roofed houses had animals stabled in the lower levels. And the streets showed evidence of the cows going off to pasture. Countryside and villages all transmitted an earthy smell, natural and homey. Dairy cattle everywhere added to the tranquility and quiet.

We paused at Samos to look down upon the huge, gray stone monastery standing solidly on the bank of the river. Still occupied by a small number of monks, it was founded in the 500s and, at one time, held an extremely important center of power, controlling two hundred towns, more than a hundred churches, and three hundred other monasteries. It was famed for its forge, farms, pharmacy, pilgrims' hospice, and schools.

We got caught in the three o'clock intense downpour, accompanied by loud thunder, and just had to walk it out. The deluge had hit about the same time the day before, but we had been cleverly snug in our albergue. We emerged from the high rock walls and dense canopy of trees into the tiny town of Aguiada and ran smack into "Helmut the Second," who we had met on the meseta where only the three of us had stayed. We had only a short reunion since he did not speak English and we did not speak German, but we were so excited to see each other again. It was silly how thrilled we were to recognize each other, when at home we might see the same people at the store or around town and never even say hello. I wondered if that summer camp mentality played a part, where those you meet in unfamiliar circumstances somehow seem more important. Do you become bonded because everyone is out of his or her comfort zone, or is it something more?

Helmut's friend spoke a bit of English and informed us that to reach the albergue at Calvor where we had planned to stay we had to backtrack twenty minutes back up hill. Disappointed, we began to trudge the remaining four kilometers into Sarria, water dripping off everything. Just then, we saw a big sign that said "Albergue: Porque no aqui?" or roughly, "Why not stay here?" This was, indeed, a good question. Without a moment's hesitation we made an immediate right turn, jumped the ditch to avoid even one extra step, and checked in. It was very nice and featured wonderful clean bathrooms. The lovely, large common room had big overstuffed couches, open-beamed, vaulted ceilings, a fireplace, and long pine tables. The host provided free hot tea, many art and photography books for perusing, and a basket full of kittens for entertainment! We met Diego, our host, who was originally from Madrid. He and his parents had built this lovely albergue a few years ago and now lived here full time. A very nice young man, Diego had been a flight attendant and had lived in America so his English was welcoming and perfect. We felt very cozy in our cocoon, sipping tea by the fire, laps full of kittens, and talking with other pilgrims as the storm continued to swirl across the landscape outside. It was another Camino miracle.

Aguiada to Portomarín
41,247 Steps, 17.57 Miles
May 9

We had a nice breakfast in the common room and played with the kittens. Outside in the covered walkway, a box on a stand contained four more adolescent-aged kittens, all snuggled in to sleep. It was the cutest thing I had seen in a long time.

"Over hill, over dale, we will hit the muddy trail, as the pilgrims go rolling along!" we sang as we walked in the pouring rain, all swathed in our full raingear again. Although rain or overcast skies followed us

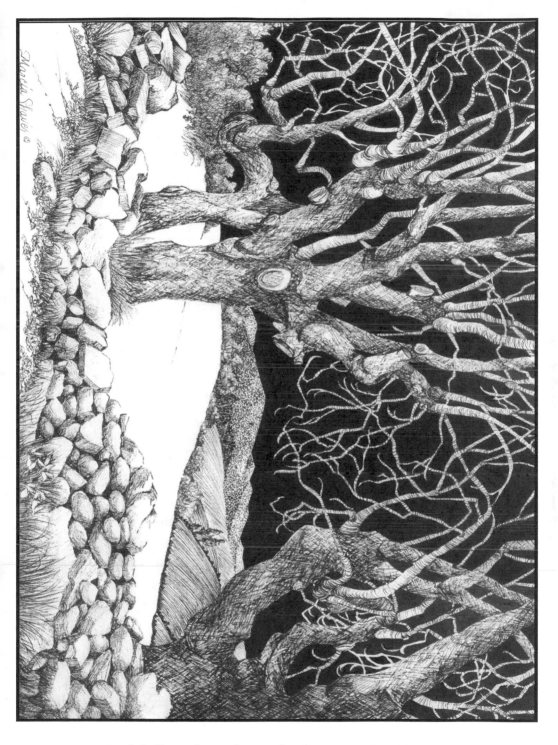

Lush hills and meadows of Galicia near Portomarin

all day, the weather made for pleasant walking. Stone fences and big, knotted, twisted trees covered in moss and ivy lined the way. They often formed a canopy above us and trailed long ribbons of ivy down over the pathway. Sheep and cattle, oblivious to the rains, filled the fields. And everywhere, there was running water, which would become one of my overriding memories of Galicia. Rainstorms obviously happened often, and the local people were prepared for it. Some areas featured elevated stones to the side of the road to walk on when it became too muddy. Other areas had large rectangular stones placed up the center of the road. When we walked on those raised stones, it was like walking through a running stream without getting your feet wet. Unbelievably, we had learned to walk on water as we drew closer to Santiago.

We reached our goal of Ferrerios around two o'clock and checked in. The moment we entered the very crowded and steamy common room, Tannis's cold went on the attack. Her sinuses slammed shut and said to her loud and clear, "If you stay here, you will contaminate everyone, plus we will not allow you to breathe for the next eighteen hours. So how long do you think you can hold your breath?" Well, what could a considerate pirigrina to do when confronted with *that*? Tannis said she did not want to feel like Jack the Ripper. I tried miserably to avoid insulting the señora by saying, "*Mi amiga esta inferma. No contaminato* everyone else. *Necessito medicamentos rapido.*" Pathetic! You would think after six weeks in Spain I could have done better.

We turned in our paper sheets, which some albergues provided as a sanitary barrier between a pilgrim and a bed that a different person slept in each night, and set off again for 9.3 kilometers (nearly five more miles) to the nearest *farmacia*. When we finally reached Portomarín at five thirty, we encountered a very steep staircase. Even though I was not the one who was sick, I whined dejectedly, "This is like facing the climb up the Aztec temple to your death! Why doesn't someone just come rip my heart out right now and get it over with?" Bravely, we pushed on to conquer the fifty-two steps. I was so tired that if there had been a sacrificial altar at the top, I might just have laid down. Fortunately for me, we traveled a Christian pilgrimage route. We eventually found a wonderful hostal with a private room and bath. We peeled off our muddy clothes and morphed into human beings again after a long, hot bath. At 6:55 we panicked, realizing the farmacia would close at 7:00. We threw on our plastic shoes and literally sprinted to the center of town. Who knew we had it in us? After our purchase of a mysterious product boldly named, "STOP COLD!" we gorged ourselves on a whole pizza each. When I asked Tannis if she was going with drugs or alcohol, she asked, "Under the circumstances, why not both?"

Portomarín to Airexe
22,946 Steps, 9.77 Miles
May 10

We had breakfast with Joakim and Reinhardt. Tannis was feeling much better due to the super cocktail of "Stop Cold," which worked muy rapido, by the way. It was another miracle.

We watched about a hundred kids in matching ponchos cross the bridge and head up the trail. We wondered if a church or school group was walking the Camino—and then wondered where they would all sleep. Hopefully, not with us. We were within the last hundred kilometers to Santiago, where one can earn the Compostela certification by just completing that short distance of sixty miles. As a result, the crowd of pilgrims had increased, and the pace had somehow changed. The newcomers to the path had a more rushed, hurry-up-and-get-it-done attitude that contrasted sharply to what we had experienced during our nearly six weeks of walking.

We hiked steadily up through dark tunnels of big trees and stone walls. When the trees opened up, we were walking on a track parallel to the road. If we looked in one direction, we saw a busy road, much traffic, and rain-slicked modern buildings. If we looked the other way, we saw verdant fields and a peaceful rural setting. The two scenes gave me pause to reflect on how we can change our perception merely by what we choose to see. Why not choose the positive side? Looking at the ugly, negative side just makes us unhappy over something we cannot change. The choice is ours and ours alone to shape our experience and affect our life.

It rained steadily all day, so hard that we could barely look up from our hoods. We reached our goal of Airexe and found a cute little place to stay in a private room over the bar. They only had two rooms, so we were very lucky. Who knows where the next private rooms might have been? We needed just one more night to get Tannis better and were grateful to have found it. So many people came after us, staggering through town with no place to stay. It was sad. I could not imagine walking the route in the high season when it is truly crowded.

We sat by a lovely, warm fire, tucked into the corner of the bar and drew. The señora provided us with bottomless cups of hot chocolate, thick and rich. Our contentment was great as we were enveloped in the embrace of the warm, crackling fire and a friendship that had become deep and natural. We talked of people who make themselves small or less than they are in order not to make others uncomfortable. They become less than they are capable of being. Tannis evoked Marianne Williamson's words, immortalized by Nelson Mandela in his freedom speech: "You are a child of God. Your playing small doesn't serve the world. There is nothing enlightening about shrinking so that other people won't feel insecure." Those good words applied to the strengths and insights we have been forging along the Camino—and to the rest of our lives.

Airexe to Casanova
28,100 Steps, 12.0 Miles
May 11

We began our day with a detour to the fourteenth century church and tenth century nunnery at Vilar de Donas. Three kilometers down a quiet country road, we came to the serene little church of El Salvador, which was the seat of the Knights of Santiago, as well as their burial place. We had come to see the famous frescos of the parable of the ten virgins and arrived exactly at the appointed opening time. It was

Endless hot chocolate, an inviting fire, and friendship in Airexe

firmly cerrado, or closed! It would not open until eleven on that day, but nobody had known that in any of the hostels, albergues, or guide-book listings. Do you think they could have put up a sign at the bar or the intersection on the main route to save the weary pilgrim before she made a six-kilometer roundtrip detour *on foot*? We were so crabby and frustrated with the Spanish schedule of everything always being closed. As we were leaving the village, we asked a man about a key, and he pointed to a white house. We walked back and found a man hav-ing his breakfast, explaining that he was a volunteer and a girl would arrive at eleven to open the church. (Yeah, right!) We put on our best dejected faces, and he relented, taking us to see the church. All the while, he was wondering why we were in such a big, fat hurry that we could not wait half an hour so he could finish his breakfast. He did not comprehend that at least one of us was very militant about taking no for an answer, and we both had no faith that anyone would show up even if we did wait until eleven. We frequently found buildings closed, opening times ignored, and nobody arriving even late to open them. One could wait all day in vain.

The gentleman relented and let us into the church. Dating from the early 1400s, the quite badly damaged frescos showed the wear over the centuries. Unique and interesting, they essentially portrayed ten different women. Apparently Christ had cautioned the virgins to behave because they could never be sure when he would be coming back. On one of the women wore the words, "You watch, and I do too." How interesting that one of the virgins appeared to be talking back to Christ. Lovely stone carvings decorated the interior, including one on the altar that looked like a castle. One sculpture on the exterior jutted out from the arches, depicting a smiling horse head. We were dutifully solemn and impressed, made a donativo, and thanked the man profusely. Just as we were leaving, the girl showed up to unlock the church, promptly at eleven. Just when you fail to believe, you are proven wrong.

We were fortunate to have the sun come out and make this corner of Galicia sparkle and shine. For a long distance, we were on quiet tracks bordered by stone walls and under tunnels of trees, which glowed with the backlighting of the sun. The terrain had turned hilly again, and the shaded pathways felt very comfortable to climb and descend on, meandering through tiny villages. Near the villages we encountered huge hand woven birdhouses with thatched roofs, raised off of the ground on stones or cement bases. Some of them were five or six feet tall, casuing speculation as to what kind of birds nested there. Each one was a unique work of art, adding interest to our immediate surroundings. Farther off, pine, oak, and chestnut trees interspersed the eucalyptus forests. We did not go far on the map, but with our detour, we traveled twelve miles and felt we had had a good day.

When we checked in to our albergue, we went upstairs to find a tiny room stuffed with men in their underwear. One was snoring loudly; one was sprawled out spread-eagle with his equipment hanging out to dry. What are you doing there, buddy, just airing them out? A distinctly male aroma permeated the room. Several other men appeared to be glaring at us for daring to make noise at three in the afternoon. We felt this was only a warm up for the night so we marched down and demanded a room for "*las mujeres solo*," or "women only." I mean seriously, there was only so much a perfumed pilgrim could take. As luck would have it, there was a second room, and we snagged bottom bunks by an open window. We then discovered a washing machine, and all was well with the world.

We discussed why we had suddenly become so crabby about the small things and realized that a distinct mental shift had occurred as we had approached Santiago. Our minds had turned to thoughts of being finished with the Camino rather than enjoying each day we still had left. We found ourselves thinking about trains, the trip home, and other details of the outside world, which we had pushed aside for the past six weeks. A new phase was about to begin. In many ways, we were so sorry for the walking to be finished. Yet, we missed our families, and we were very tired physically. We welcomed the rest that would come with the completion of our journey and looked forward to the reunion with loved ones. The Camino taught us to live in the present moment well, and we welcomed taking each day as it came to us without worry or fear. We vowed to make the most of our last few days and take that lesson home with us. So frequently we worry about events far in the

Hand woven bird houses near Casanova

future or circumstances over which we have no control, thus squandering the present. Trying to live each moment well was a challenge we would try to accept from that time forward.

There was no restaurant in Casanova, so we were told to be outside at six. The owner of the restaurant, just one kilometer away, would pick us up, take us home and feed us dinner. Cries of, "Great," "*Fantastico,*" "*Geweldie,*" "*Wunderbar,*" and "Brilliant" greeted this news! Promptly at six, we were parked on the bench, lined up like hungry birds, salivating in anticipation under the wisteria. At six fifteen, a woman in a tiny car rolled up, followed by frantic gesturing and shoving pirigrinos into the backseat that was already half filled with boxes. She stuffed in exactly two people. Ha ha ha. Oh well, it was only one kilometer away, so we knew she would be back in a flash to get the remaining ten people. Fifteen minutes went by, and we realized these must be Spanish kilometers that are always longer than stated. She finally returned, minus the boxes, and we stuffed another five people in. She was gone fifty minutes, and we were about to gnaw the arms off the chairs, but we were too weak from malnutrition to attempt it as we sat in the gathering darkness. It had been many kilometers and many hours since breakfast. We speculated on what the heck she must have been doing, cooking the dinner herself? When she arrived, we all made a mad dash for the car. In completely un-pilgrim-like fashion, nobody was willing to wait one minute longer to be gracious. We played contortionist and all fit in, with the help of a little olive oil. I had only one cheek on the seat and a death grip on the overhead handle in case the door flew open and ejected me. We were ripping along a pot-holed dirt road, every light on the dashboard was flashing like a Las Vegas casino, and the car was riding on its rims. Three minutes later we arrived at our destination. Hummm, very puzzling. Had she just forgotten us earlier? We joined the first groups and discovered that they had not yet been served dinner but were well into the wine. It soon became apparent that the enterprising señora *was* doing it all, while her sweet but useless husband looked on. We determined that on the first trip she had been on her way home from the *supermercado*, and the boxes contained our dinner. She picked up a few people, chopped the salads, put the meat in the oven, picked up a few more people, set the tables and cooked dessert, picked up the last group, seated us all, served dinner, prepared the bills, then drove us back. It took forever for dinner, but it was so much fun we lost our irritation and let the evening happen. In addition to many people we already knew from our weeks on the Camino, we met a couple from Holland, Marika from Germany, Ron, Robbie, and Sarah from Australia, and a woman from Vienna. We laughed and shared the most excellent dinner and wine until ten thirty. It was past lockup when we returned, and we had to sneak stealthily into our bunks. The señora had worked her tail off, and we all left her a massive tip. She was so concerned because it was too much money, and she did not know who had overpaid. I told her in my inadequate Spanish that the money was hers to keep for all of her hard work, and she got tears in her eyes. I hope she makes her fortune and gets to buy a big new van. She most certainly worked harder than humanly possible and deserved all good things to flow her way.

Casanova to Ribadiso do Baixo
31,833 Steps, 13.56 Miles
May 12

We started out in a downpour so it was back to the pantalones plastico. Jan, a Dutch pilgrim, shared coffee with us, so that gave us some fuel until we reached the first bar. Everyone we had just said good-bye to was there for a big breakfast, so we had a wonderful meal.

The sun lingered just above the diffused clouds, occasionally peeking through to reveal a hundred different shades of green in the landscape. It was a perfect temperature for walking, steadily up and down hill all day as we crossed at least six mini-mountains and river valleys. The eucalyptus trees gave a beautiful scent to the air and intermingled with oaks, pines, and some beech to shelter us as we traveled the quiet country lanes. Farmers were cutting the green pastures for hay, and gardens flourished everywhere with potatoes, lettuce, cabbage, and peppers. We saw lemon trees so laden with fruit that they had to have their branches supported. The stone fences contained abundant sheep, dairy cattle, and horses with new foals that were ever-present symbols of the fertility of Galicia.

We reached Melide and passed on the famous octopus restaurants. Just outside the town, we came to a tiny but beautiful Romanesque church, built in the 1100s. It was, of course, cerrado. I asked around the village, and Tannis sulked on a bench. Jeez! She was really serious about "No more detours and no more churches." However, I prevailed. A tiny, shriveled, stooped-over señora in a print apron and black dress, fashionably accessorized with support hose, crept down the one-block village with the keys and her hand cleverly out for a donativo. We passed Tannis still pouting on the bench, and I actually had to do a head jerk to get her to go to the church. There was no way she was passive-aggressively not going to look, especially after my thirty-minute crawl through the village with the señora. I reminded her, I must confess, in a grossly superior way about our vow to live each moment well. She relented, and we went in to see some unusual and beautiful frescoes, and very much worth our while. Lovely black and white patterns bordered the artwork and contained figures very lifelike, not stiff and stylized as was typical of the time. The best part was the maze of pattern that made our eyes shift, nearly identical to the M. C. Escher designs, which were thought to be revolutionary eight hundred years later! It seemed to support the theory that nothing is truly new in art. It was very exciting to think what a stir those frescoes must have created so very long ago.

At last we crossed a medieval bridge and came to our albergue at Ribadiso do Baixo, right on the banks of the Río Iso. It was the most beautiful albergue we had stayed in, composed of a collection of stone buildings. Originally an old pilgrims' hospice, it had been restored and modernized, winning an environmental architecture award in the process. The bathrooms were a stroll away, and the kitchen was on two levels with a tiny stone door connecting the sections. The bright blue paint of the heavy wooden doors and window casings gave a lively contrast to the terra cotta tile roofs. Large pieces of stone framed the doorways and windows and appeared randomly in the walls. Between the stones, a mosaic of small rocks in a multitude of colors filled every space. They ranged in color from cream to deep iron red, dark burnt umber through yellowish raw sienna, dove gray to a soft pinkish violet. Gray cobblestone courtyards united all the buildings. It retained the feeling of a linked community, sitting in a quiet stretch of meadowland along the river.

We ended the day by sharing dinner with a delightful couple from Australia, Ron and Robbie. Originally, a Dutch couple shared our table as well. Our conversation drifted toward the spiritual, and the Dutch woman told us in a very sincere way, "My husband knows he is not the first person in my life. Christ is the first, as it should be. Walking through the mountains, with all the spring flowers, is like walking through a bouquet. It was my wedding bouquet, and I was the bride of Christ." She then turned to Tannis and asked, "You are a Christian?" Uh-oh, Pagan Alert! She *would* have to ask Tannis, who is so innocent and honest all the time. I would have just said yes and let it go at that, *but no!* Tannis had to elaborate, saying, "I think there are a lot of religions that have merit." The more she talked, the deeper the woman frowned. Her husband was hiding under the table by that time, making shushing noises. Ron and Robbie were checking out the ceiling. I finally kicked Tannis hard enough to have her pause to say, "Owww!" At that point the Dutch couple excused themselves and huffed off, never to speak to us again.

Full of the "Rah-rah, go team go" fun-loving attitude of many Australians, Ron and Robbie poured the wine and entertained us the rest of the night, lightening an awkward situation. They regaled us with tales of their trek over the Route Napoleon just a few days after it had been closed for us, and many other interesting stories. They were totally enjoying themselves on their journey, people-lovers to the core. They provided such amusing company; we felt as if we had known them for a long time. Such a gift they gave us, making strangers feel so comfortable and laugh late into the night.

Restored pilgrim's hospice at Ribadiso

Ribadiso do Baixo to Arca
34,894 Steps, 14.83 Miles
May 13

Swathed in plastico again, we set out in a mist and drizzle that reminded us of the Northwest. It was a really beautiful walk. All day the sun peeked in and out, and we constantly stripped to T-shirts then returned to rain gear. The roses were bursting forth in their prime, and we reflected on our journey as we passed the day. We talked of all we had seen and who we had become, enjoying one of our last days on the Camino to the fullest.

Huge, gnarled trees with interlocking branches bordered the trails. Tall ferns and flowers blanketed the earth at their feet. When we emerged from the forests, neat stone homes greeted us. Nearly each one featured a unique *horreo*, or corncrib, used to dry and store the harvest. Some were very old and simple while others were very decorative and ornate. All sat raised above the ground several feet and skirted by lush grasses and flowers.

Newer homes dotting the hillsides became more frequent, and finally we reached the nondescript town of Arca do Pino. A modern looking suburb, it had one of the main roads to Santiago running through its center. Since it was within a day's walk of Santiago, many pilgrims stay in Arca for convenience, even though it lacks charm or any historical significance. The albergue featured ice-cold showers and no shower curtains in a co-ed bathroom. We actually let out blood-curdling screams when the water hit us. We just stood there and got clean, despite the glacial temperature, as two young Spanish women stood guard and acted as our shower curtains. After emerging the icy blast, men shaving at the sinks gave us a thumbs up and said, "*Brava! Muy fuerta!*" which loosely translated means, "You are brave and very strong!" Of course we laughed our brains out when the Spanish women screamed just as loudly when the water hit them! We bonded, shivering, as we compared how blue our bodies had become. What a shock that was after a long, sweaty walk through the mountains.

"Horreo", or corn crib near Arca

We were able to get dinner at six rather than the customary eight thirty, so we celebrated with a bottle of Vino Tinto and ice cream sundaes to die for. They were served in fluted glasses eight inches across and topped with a mountain of whipped cream. The finale was a cookie wafer artfully tucked into the side, with shaved chocolate and a cherry on top. Symbolic of our attitude shift on the Camino, our choice showed that we thought nothing of obtaining a balanced food grouping of fruit, carbohydrates, and protein by consuming an entire bottle of wine and gargantuan ice cream sundaes for our dinner. When I could not possibly eat another bite, Tannis snatched my sundae and asked, "Are you gonna eat that?" just a millisecond before she inhaled it. The best part was that we did not feel even a trace of guilt!

We returned to the albergue to prepare for an early start in the morning. We had less than twenty kilometers, or twelve miles, to our goal. I could not believe it. Tomorrow we would walk into Santiago with mixed feelings and a lot of pride.

Arca to Santiago de Compostela
34,368 Steps, 14.64 Miles
May 14

As we walked toward Santiago, the sun was rising, a pale pink, behind the eucalyptus forests. The scent of early morning dew and eucalyptus, white flowering shrubs that smelled like gardenias, and the earthy scent of the fields combined to form the perfume of beautiful Galicia. The eucalyptus trees had trunks colored a mixture of soft rose, warm tan, and grayed green, blended in and out of each other. The silvery leaves shifted, shimmering in the breeze, and long strips of brick-colored bark padded the pathway under foot. The walk through the forests lasted much longer than we had anticipated this close to the city.

We soon hit the top of the hill at Monte de Gozo and were disappointed that we could not see the cathedral spires as tradition promised. At that distance, the trees and city obscured the view, and further into the city, the buildings were too close to us. We trudged on for what seemed like forever, realizing that the kilometer markers declaring our arrival in Santiago stopped at the outskirts of town, leaving several more miles through busy traffic to navigate, quite a shock after the tranquility of the countryside. When we reached the city center, we went directly to get our Compostela Certificates before the office closed for siesta. The woman reviewed all of the albergue stamps on our Pilgrim's Credential, which symbolized our journey as we made our way across Spain, and looked at me in disbelief. Then she smiled as she handed me my Compostela and said, "Congratulations!" Congratulations, indeed. We had arrived in Santiago. We had walked over five hundred miles. We had driven our bodies to their limits. And we would never be the same.

We picked up our packages from the post office that we had mailed in Burgos, which seemed an eon ago. Our things had arrived safely, another Camino miracle, and were like Christmas presents waiting to be opened. In our cute little hotel room, we cleaned up, found what seemed like a whole new wardrobe of shoes and skirts and tights, and dressed to go to church.

The cathedral impressed us both with its size and grandeur, looming huge and dark against the gray skies. We entered the cathedral through the eighteenth-century doors that were part of a façade built at that time, enclosing the original twelfth-century Romanesque entryway. These carvings on the original portico, or entry, are a masterpiece known as the "Entrance of Glory." The sculptures were quite beautiful, fluid and lifelike, a testament to the skill and genius of Maestro Mateo, who designed and built it between 1168 and 1188. In the center of the portico the hands of countless pilgrims over nearly a thousand years had touched the tree of Jesse and worn a cave-like depression. Lastly, we went behind the altar to participate in the tradition of hugging the thirteenth-century, life-sized, gold and jewel-encrusted statue of St. James. As I closed my eyes and laid my cheek against the golden cloak of Santiago's back, I had a spiritual revelation. At first, it left me completely cold, and I felt a vacant place in my heart. I thought, "The cathedral and art represent a stunning achievement for the architects and the artisans. But does it inspire me to fall on my knees at the glory of God? No, it is not for me. The rituals and the gold, the power and the rules, they provide a cohesive force and a comfort to many people, which is wonderful. But it is not for me."

Then what do I believe? In a moment of crystal clear silence, I received an answer loud and clear. It was what I had always believed intuitively—in the journey, not the grand destination. No manmade structure could hold a candle to the fields full of wildflowers, the trees reaching sculpturally toward the sky, the clear-running streams, and the rocky hillsides. The green pastures and mountains we had traversed each day under the sunrises and sunsets painted across the vault of heaven were truly the hand of a Supreme Being. Each day was a resurrection. The baby animals with their mothers were a miracle each and every time. They are the future. Every meal was a communion. We had been walking through paradise and creation itself. God was all around us and within our hearts, not just in the cathedral so grand and huge. Yet here beneath us lay the bones of St. James, one of the twelve apostles who walked with Jesus. Above us stood the image of gentle Santiago Perigrino covered in scallop shells, smiling down at us from his niche in the cathedral wall above the final door of pardon and forgiveness, welcoming us to the end of our journey and validating all that we had discovered within ourselves.

Santiago
9,145 Steps, 3.9 Miles
May 15

We luxuriously slept until seven thirty before heading to the bar for breakfast. Tannis inhaled three doughnuts, a mini ham-and-cheese sandwich, two cookies and two grande café con leches. She was ravenous and could not seem to get full, and I was only one doughnut and one cookie behind her. This was confirmed when we went swimsuit shopping for our trip to the spa. Donde esta Tannis's breasts? *Desaparecido!* They had disappeared! *El Vanisho!* Do we have to go breast shopping as well? It is amazing how tired and hungry our bodies are. After the

"Santiago Peregrino", or Saint James the Pilgrim

excitement of the pilgrims' mass, we felt justified in ordering an extravagant seafood feast for two and a bottle of the local white wine. Lunch arrived, accompanied by two baskets of bread, on an eighteen-inch platter heaped with lobster, two kinds of crab, mussels, clams, razor clams, and several delicacies that we did not have a clue about. No problem! We got down to the serious business of gluttony and ordered dessert before we headed back for a siesta. We then shopped for two hours, at which time we had expended enough energy and euros over all of three blocks that we felt justified in eating once again. In true Spanish style, we feasted on those great, tasty, heavy snacks, tapas. Of course, as tapas are only appetizers, we had dinner at ten thirty.

We attended the pilgrims' mass at noon. It was standing room only. The cathedral held seating for over a thousand, so probably two or three thousand people had packed into the church. Many pilgrims had just arrived and still wore their packs. It was strange to see all of those people who walked the Camino at the same time we had, or within a day of our passage, and we saw only half a dozen familiar faces. It gave us a sense of how many pilgrims had passed the same way, nameless, yet commonly bonded by experience. Pleasingly, a nun conducted much of the service. She read the names of each of the countries represented, how many pilgrims had arrived from each one, and where they had begun walking. A handful of people had walked the 620-mile Silver Route from Sevilla, and three had begun in LePuy, France, walking an additional 500 miles. With the exception of those few, we had walked just as far or farther than every pilgrim represented, over 550 miles. We had probably taken twice as many steps as someone taller. And, amazingly, we were the only two Americans—two tough little pirigrinas. I was so proud of Tannis and me and what we had accomplished that my heart got caught in my throat and tears filled my eyes. A nun with an exceptionally strong, pure voice filled the cathedral with hauntingly beautiful melodies, sung without accompaniment. Then the massive organ began to play, sending truly magnificent music throughout the church. The priests lit the botafumeiro, one of the largest silver incense burners in the Catholic world, and it began to swing slowly in an arc, the smoke wafting out into the air. As the priests continued to draw

"Botofumerio", in incense burner, in the Santiago cathedral

back on the ropes and pulleys, the arc grew wider and wider, until the botafumeiro nearly reached the high, vaulted ceilings. It made a whooshing sound like the wings of angels as it rose and fell through the air directly over our heads. Just as it reached its apex, a ray of brilliant sunshine poured in through the upper windows and set the smoke-filled air ablaze with shafts of light. It indelibly placed a mystical seal on the finale of our pilgrimage.

Santiago to Finisterre
Bus Plus 40,236 Steps, 17.13 Miles
May 16-20

The bus ride to Finisterre was spectacular. We crossed over lush green mountains then skirted the coast. Large sculptural rocks interspersed the beautiful white sand beaches. The hillsides spilled down to the sea and cradled small colorful villages. Fishing boats bobbed gently on the sparkling blue Atlantic waters. Overhead, big, fluffy, white clouds skittered across the blue sky, lit by the sunshine. In that truly magical part of the world, we spent the next four days resting and collecting our thoughts.

We had felt a sad and vacant spot in our hearts when we did not see Marjorie and Elaine, or many others, in Santiago. However, as our days passed in Finisterre, we saw Ron and Robbie from Australia, Yasukiro and his father from Japan, Reinhardt and Yoakhim, and several of the German women from the breast cancer study group. We had a very sincere and touching email from Paulo thanking all of his Camino friends for their support and blessings, saying "When I go up the thirty-three steps to the cathedral, as I cross the door, I will bring you in my heart." Terttu later said, "My heart beats differently still." We learned that Atilla had waited for his bride, Marjorie, on the steps of the cathedral until she arrived. And best of all, who showed up to bring our journey full circle but Martien? He had been an integral part of our Camino, and spending the last few days in his company felt like a satisfying completion. The last time we had seen him, he was standing

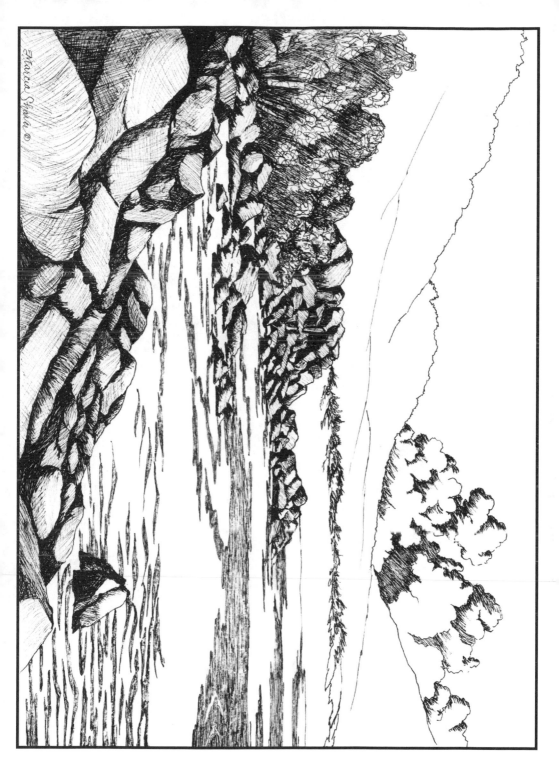

The costa del morte near Finisterre

at the bus stop in his red fleece, waving us a farewell with a happy smile on his face. It felt right to know so many different ways to live life are good. One way does exclude another. Many equally valid paths lead to the same destination.

During our stay, we made several treks to the faro, or lighthouse. The cliffs plunged vertically to the ocean, covered in a carpet of white daisies, yellow broom, and pink foxgloves. The sea ranged from a steely blue to a brilliant emerald green, the shallows an incredible turquoise. Huge, golden, creamy rocks formed outcroppings that sheltered small beaches. At the lighthouse, we reached the Camino de Santiago marker 0.00 kilometers, scallop shell pointing downward to signify the end, with the cobalt sea as a backdrop. We had walked to the end of the earth. It was a powerful place, where once the Phoenicians worshipped the sun god, Ara Solis. The Celtic people held important fertility rituals here, and the Romans came here to watch the sea swallow the sun. On clear nights, a band of small clouds often sat on the far western horizon. The light, brilliant on the sea, formed luminous patterns and mirror-like reflections. The low clouds burned with intense golds, pinks, orange, and platinum as the sun sank behind them. You could almost hear the sizzle when the sun slipped into the sea. From the eastern skies at your back, Mother Moon took her place in a cool field of blues, lavender, and mauve in a moment like no other. For thousands of years, the various peoples had believed the sun was extinguished in these waters each night and wondered if it would rise again. Beyond the horizon lay the feared place of darkness, monsters, and the vast unknown. According to their beliefs, this marked the western-most point on the continent of Europe. It must have taken great courage for the explorers five hundred years ago to set sail into this region of legend and superstition. Imagine their surprise when they discovered the Americas. They had encountered no landfall between that very point and North America. It was a wild, beautiful, thought-provoking place. It was the end. It was the beginning. It was the unknown.

Even to this day people follow the Way of St. James to this spot and hold cleansing rituals symbolic of death and rebirth. Some burn their boots or clothes. Marjorie and Elaine burned their bras. Some

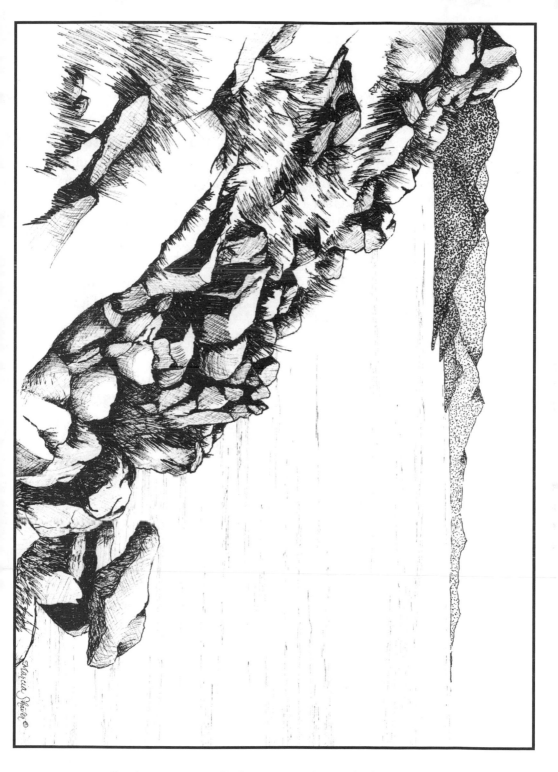

"Cabo Finisterre", the cape at the end of the earth

pilgrims leave thoughts, crosses, or pictures. Others write, and some, like Tannis and I, draw. I sat cradled in a warm rock pocket, perched above the cliffs plunging into the turbulent Atlantic, with the sun on my face and a gentle breeze stirring the wildflowers. It was a good place to reflect on this artist's journey. It had been a gift of time, not to worry about anything. We had had a journey with great continuity, walking across an entire country. This seemed a fitting place to complete our epic, when there was nowhere else to go, as we had reached land's end.

We had been so very fortunate, Tannis and I. Really the perfect person to walk with, she was gentle, considerate, tough, intuitive, willing to stop or go on as needed, and cheerful. I truly believed it was meant to be.

It felt strange to be at the end of the journey. We had met some incredible and interesting people. In the open spirit of the Camino, we made friends who would never have been friends at home. We had always begun with a polite attitude of respect for others and assumed they would show us their best side. Our hearts connect to people from all over our world, and we will forever think of that big world in a more personal and intimate way. The wonderful people of Spain embraced us. With kindness, helpfulness, honesty, and a sincere pride in their country, they shared their home with us. We experienced so much simple joy and laughter, so much touching of hearts, and so much beauty. Those parts I will treasure forever.

We had walked many miles and seen things that we had never even dreamed of. We had watched spring unfold, retreat back into winter, and blossom again. We had traversed the evolving countryside, its bounty unfolding quietly around us. We had felt every hill, every plain, and every mountain. We had smelled every flower, the clean scent of the rain in the air, the freshly turned soil in the early morning, and the earthy aroma of the animals in the fields. We had encountered history and art in the villages and cities, as well as in the most unexpected country lanes.

Our bodies had been tested and pushed to their limits. I hoped I had not done permanent damage to my feet, as they ached and tingled constantly with an intensity that was hard to bear. Tannis had lost so much weight she looked like a skeleton as she limped along on her bad knee. We had also gained so much strength that our muscles felt like rocks. We would never again question whether we could make it to our goal. Like the iron of this region, the journey had forged us into something stronger. At the same time, it had expanded our spirits as they had evolved. They had quieted yet had become richer for all that they had received. A gentle shift in perspective had left me feeling a softer, better person on the inside. Spirit and body had both triumphed.

We turned our thoughts toward home, finished with walking and ready to put a final seal on our journey. Although a nightmare at times, the way had been a dream come true. It had exceeded our wildest expectations, and for that, I thanked my kind husband from the bottom of my heart. He had made this possible for me, staying at home, working, and taking care of all of the responsibilities that we usually share. I thought of that each day with profound gratitude.

What gifts we have been given!

Equipment

Hiking Boots

Your feet will take the most abuse so it is imperative that you plan as carefully as possible for your footwear. My original plan for training was to walk with my fully loaded pack for ten miles a day, each day, for the three weeks prior to departure. Due to a pulled Achilles tendon six weeks before departure, I did not follow that wise plan. For the first three days of walking, my feet were tired but fine. On the fourth day, I began to have a series of problems that plagued me for the entire journey. The moral to the story is that you need not only to break in your boots (I did!); you also need to walk many miles in them **with a fully loaded pack** every day for at least a week. Carrying the added weight over an extended period of time can change your feet! Believe me. And if your feet swell enough that the boots become too tight, get a new pair of boots in a bigger size before you leave home. Repeat the loaded-pack scenario. You do not want to have feet so sore that they prevent you from finishing the Camino.

Look for the following qualities in a boot:

1. Lightweight and breathable: remember every ounce of boot has to be lifted every step of the way!

2. A good stiff sole to protect your feet from rocky trails and uneven surfaces

3. Waterproof Gore-Tex construction to keep your feet dry and allow air circulation.

4. Ankle-high tops to give support and keep the water out.

Other shoes

If you opt to take sandals to wear off the trail, make sure they have a padded foot bed and adjustable straps to allow for swelling.

A pair of plastic Crocs, or clogs, is perfect. They are loose fitting enough to allow for swelling or to wear with socks. The foot bed is cushioned and they weigh next to nothing. They dry instantly, and you can even wear them in the shower if you choose to.

Socks

It is important to have a couple pairs of socks of different thicknesses so that you can adjust for more boot space. I chose Thorlo hiking socks with a fabric content of 58 percent CoolMax, 23 percent acrylic, 14 percent stretch nylon, and 5 percent Spandex. Get one lightweight pair, two moderately cushioned pairs, and one thick cushioned pair. Remember to fit your boots while wearing your heaviest sock and still allow some extra room for potential swelling of your feet.

The following features are important:

1. Moisture-wicking fabric to help your feet stay dry and cool.

2. Cushioning in the heel and ball of the foot to cut down on blisters, impact, and bruising.

3. A lighter padding in the instep and arch, with added elastic support, than in the bottom of the sock on the ball of the foot and heel.

Alternative boot foot bed liner

If you wear orthopedic liners, get a special pair made with extra padding in the heel and ball of the foot in addition to the corrective structure.

If you do not wear orthopedic liners, you can pick up a pair of gel inserts at the pharmacy. Alternate them with the liners that come in your boots to provide your feet with variety and comfort.

Trekking Poles

Almost everyone on the Camino uses trekking poles. They are of great assistance to your knees and ankles while going up and down hills, as well as a useful aid in balancing your pack weight.

I like the Black Diamond Compact lightweight model. They telescope to twenty-four inches in length, allowing them to be stowed in your pack for transport. The latching mechanism for securing the pole in the extended position is easy to use and extremely secure. The handles are made of a soft, secure gripping material. The straps are very soft, comfortable, and do not rub. It is a good idea to purchase the optional rubber tips for the ends so that you do not drive yourself crazy with the clickity-clickity-click sound they make on pavement.

Trekking poles will have to be checked, along with your pocket-knife, for the flight.

Pack

Remember that your pack is your friend. The most important feature to consider is a well-constructed frame that fits your body. It is worth the extra money to go to a store like REI that has knowledgeable sales people to assist in a proper fit. It should be waterproof and have many adjustments. Learn how every feature works and every strap adjusts before you begin your trip. My pack is a Gregory Jade 50. This means it is designed for a woman and holds 50 liters or 3050 cubic inches. It will hold everything you need, and a bigger pack is just going to tempt you to take more. It weighs 3 pounds and is made of rip-stop nylon with very versatile compartments and waterproof zippers. There is a built-in "camelback" for water so you will not need an additional water bottle.

If you are traveling in winter or spring, you might consider a rain cover for your pack. Mine weighs only 3 oz. and was well worth purchasing and carrying in order to arrive with dry clothes and sleeping bag after a very wet hike. I kept it in an outside pack pocket and used it to sit on at rest stops.

A scallop shell signifying that you are a pilgrim to be tied to the outside of your pack can be purchased at the beginning of your journey in St. Jean Pied de Port for one or two euros.

Water Bottle or Hydration System

My pack had a "camel back" hydration system, which included a flexible plastic bladder for water or other liquids, with a tube attached that fit over my shoulder, so that I could drink without having to access a water bottle. This worked great, but some people prefer a water bottle. If you do not have a favorite container, you don't need anything fancy. You can just buy a plastic bottle of water when you arrive and refill it as necessary. The water in Spain is clean, and there are many public fountains along the way labeled "potable." Whatever system you choose, keep it in an accessible area of your pack so that you can reach it while walking without "unsaddling."

Sleeping Bag/ Sleep Sack

You do not need both a sleeping bag and a silk sleep sack, but many albergues do not have blankets so you will definitely need one. In summer, the lighter sleep sack is probably enough. However, I hate to be cold, especially when I am trying to sleep, so I purchased a Mountain Hardware Ultralamina 32 mummy-style sleeping bag. It weighs 1.5 pounds and is warm down to 32 degrees F. On the few nights when this was not enough, I slept in my clothes or found an extra blanket. I stuffed it into an extra small "Sea to Summit" waterproof bag with compression straps. The dimensions with the sleeping bag stuffed inside were 12 inches long by 6 inches wide. This compact size allowed me to carry the sleeping bag inside the bottom of my pack for added protection from the elements.

The Portable Bathroom

It is strange that along the entire Camino de Santiago we only found one public restroom, and that one was locked. (We suspected Martien was in there.) In Spain it is acceptable, even expected, that you will use the restrooms in the bars. They are designated servicios or WCs. However, this frequently leads to café con leche, which leads to the need to stop at the next bar. This may be a clever Spanish marketing technique coordinated by enterprising bar owners, but it can make for uncomfortable walking between stops.

Obviously, when you have to go, you just have to go regardless of where you are. It is a sad fact that many people use the side of the trail, as evidenced by the toilet paper. We were raised with the Pacific Northwest "leave no trace" philosophy, so we invented the simple concept of the portable bathroom:

> Put several plastic zip-lock sandwich bags into your pack for the duration of the trip. Each morning make sure one bag has toilet paper in it, and keep it in an outside pocket of your pack for easy access. If you absolutely must use the side of the trail, pick up your paper and anything else you have left. Seal it in the bag to be disposed of properly when you reach the next bathroom. This simple courtesy will be greatly appreciated by fellow pilgrims as well as enhancing the aesthetics of the Camino.

Outer Clothing

If you are traveling in summer, the weather will be very hot and dry all the way from Pamplona to Galicia, sometimes exceeding 115 degrees. However, the Pyrenees and Galicia can be cool and wet any time of the year. Personally, I would not like to walk the Camino in summer because of the higher temperatures and larger numbers of travelers who create more crowded conditions in the albergues. However, if you do choose to walk in the summer, you probably will not need a sleeping bag, a fleece jacket, gloves, and rain pants, and possibly not even a lightweight jacket.

In spring and fall, a light fleece jacket and a light wind jacket with a hood are just right. Even on windy days, you will be quite warm, layered up, because you are exercising and carrying a pack. For a winter trek, follow the same principle with slightly heavier weights in fleece and jacket. My complete set up included:

1. "REI Elements" (Recreational Equipment, Inc.) women's jacket weighs 12 oz. and is made of a breathable, waterproof, windproof fabric. It has zippered underarm vents, a detachable hood with a drawstring for tightening it around your face, and zippered side and front pockets. The length drops just below my bottom and has a drawstring. The cuffs have elastic and a Velcro closure. All these features make for a snug, comfortable, versatile, windproof, and mostly waterproof outer layer.

2. The lightest possible weight, long-sleeved polar fleece jacket with a full zipper down the front. When combined with the rain jacket, it is very warm, even for a freeze chicken like me! My Land's End Therma Check fleece has zippered pockets and weighs 8 oz.

3. A pair of breathable, water- and wind-proof pants with zippers and a drawstring at the bottom. They should have an elastic waist and pockets with waterproof zippers. Mine weigh 7 oz. and are made of 100% nylon. These are not necessary in summer and fall.

4. A very light-weight pair of gloves is recommended unless you are traveling in summer. REI sells an Oslo Liner glove that is perfect. The fabric is a polyester/wool blend that wicks moisture, dries quickly, stays warm even when wet, breathes, keeps out most drafts, and weighs only 1 oz. for the pair.

5. Everyone needs a hat to keep the sun and weather off the face. I took a baseball cap made of a quick-drying fabric. In summer you will need a hat that shades your ears and neck as well as your face. Additionally, I had an OR brand wind-stopper, fleece ski hat that was fantastic and weighed only 1.5 ounces. I could wear both hats at the same time if necessary, in addition to my hood. Obviously summer travel does not require the ski hat.

6. A Buff or a scarf. Personally, I think a Buff is much more versatile than a scarf. It is a stretchy, soft, moisture wicking, lightweight tube of fabric about 20 inches around and 18 inches long. It can be worn as a scarf around your neck, as a headband, wristband, mask, hair band, balaclava, ponytail scrunchy, pirate-style hat, a cap, or whatever else you can think of. (The skinny girls even wear them as tank tops or skirts.) I used mine on my arm, from the armpit to the elbow, for about ten days because I had developed a pack rub there, and it protected my sore spot without being hot or cumbersome. They are sold at sporting goods stores or on the Web at www. Buff.us. Appropriately, mine was manufactured in Spain.

Other Clothes

I purchased Exofficio travel underwear and sports bras that would dry as fast as possible. I took three pairs of underwear: one to wear hiking, one to change into after a shower at the destination, and one to wash each night. This could have been done with two pairs, but there were times when laundry did not dry so an extra pair was nice.

I took three Exofficio T-shirts: one to wear, one to change into while the dirty one was being washed, and one to sleep in. They weighed only 2 oz. each and dried quickly. I rotated the sleeping T-shirt with the other two for a little variety. I slept in the T-shirt and silk boxer shorts because I wanted to be somewhat covered in the communal sleeping areas.

I walked in my stretchy yoga pants (Sugoi brand) every single day because they were so comfortable, did not bind, dried very quickly, and were perfect for layering with the wind/rain pants. The Exofficio brand travel pants and the skirt were more dressy yet still comfortable and acceptable for walking around in the towns and cities. Many people take the lightweight travel pants with zip-off legs so that they have shorts for warmer days.

The one long-sleeved Exofficio travel shirt was fantastic. I wore it as a sunshade, a light jacket when the windbreaker or fleece was too much, and layered it with the T-shirts when it was cold.

Accessories and Toiletries

Keep these to a minimum in both size and what you choose to take. Buy travel size toothpaste, toothbrush, shampoo, dental floss, sunscreen, ibuprofen or aspirin, soap. Take only a few Band-Aids, a small pair of nail clippers, and a set of tweezers for basic first aid. A razor, hair band, one ChapStick, and any personal prescription medications you take should complete your list. Anything else you can imagine, you can buy in Spain. Ladies, you do not need makeup or a hairdryer.

A good pair of sunglasses will save your eyes from fatigue in the sunny Spanish countryside. I have Smith glasses with lenses that change quickly for brighter or darker days, and although this is not really necessary, the spare lenses weigh nothing. They have a lightweight yet rigid case, which is large enough to fit my reading glasses into as well. If you wear prescription glasses it might be a good idea to take along a spare paper prescription so that you can replace them if they get lost or broken.

A very small, lightweight towel that will dry quickly is very important. Regular towels are bulky and not only can remain damp; they can get everything else in your pack wet as well.

A basic sewing kit with basic thread colors, one needle, and several safety pins will come in handy. Buttons invariably fall off and seams rip out at the most inconvenient times. This serves a double purpose in treating blisters.

A mini flashlight or a tiny headlight is very useful in the group sleeping quarters. When the lights are out, you need to be able to find your possessions or make your way safely and quietly to the bathroom without disturbing others more than necessary. I have a Tikka brand headlight with a high, low, and flashing function. Low beam is best for reading or finding things in your bunk. The high beam is useful if you happen to get caught on the trail after dark. The flashing function lets you be seen by cars and other traffic if you are walking in a busy area near twilight or after dark.

You will also need a pocketknife and a plastic "spork," or spoon and fork combination, for cutting up picnic food and eating on the trail.

A good pair of earplugs is absolutely mandatory if you want to sleep at all! Additionally, I carried a small alarm clock that had glow-in-the-dark numbers so that if I did wake up I knew if it was midnight or five in the morning. It helps me to go back to sleep if I know how much time I have before everyone begins to get up for the day.

A lightweight, nylon, shoulder-bag style purse or backpack is very useful. I had a Kiva nylon bag that weighs only 1 or 2 oz., could be comfortably worn across my back or used as a purse, and held quite a lot. Whenever we left our packs in the albergues, we took with us the following items that we might need in town: money, passport, credit cards, phone, camera, and drawing materials. On the few days that we put our packs on the mochila transport service, I carried it as a daypack with my picnic lunch and water bottle in addition to those items.

Phone

I purchased an international phone from Mobal that has no monthly fee and a permanent phone number with voice mail. It is expensive to use by the minute but enabled my family members at home to feel that they could contact me in case of a dire emergency. I checked each day to see if I had an emergency message, which was free. We also used it a couple of times to call home when we could not find a public phone.

For calls home, buy a phone card for five euros at almost any bar in Spain. This is by far the least expensive way to talk to home, and there are still public phones in many bars and public places. It has been my experience that the phone cards you purchase in America do not work in Europe, even though they claim to.

Camera equipment

I took a digital camera with two extra memory chips and a charger for the battery. I took the extra battery so that I would have a spare if mine died in the middle of the day or if I was unable to charge it for several days in a row. You can download your images to a CD in many Internet cafés along the way and erase them from your chip, but the extra memory chips weighed next to nothing. I did not want to risk loosing my images, and the extra chips are smaller than a CD anyway. I had a padded, somewhat waterproof case that I attached to the outside of my pack belt for easy access on the trail. I kept the memory chips, extra battery, and charger in a zip-lock bag for extra waterproofing.

Currency Adaptor

Any travel store can sell you a plug that adapts the European electric current to one that is safe for American cell phone and battery chargers. You will also need an adapter that converts the US style plug ends to the 2 pronged outlets found in Europe. They are small and inexpensive, and you only need one adaptor for all of your accessories that need to be plugged in.

Guidebooks to the Camino

I consider two guidebooks most useful:

A Pilgrim's Guide to the Camino de Santiago , St. Jean Pied de Port-Santiago de Compostela by John Brierley

> This very up-to-date book lists all of the albergues, hostals, hotels and other places to stay along the way. It also contains detailed maps, in-depth walking instructions, distances between towns, elevation gains, historical information, and recommendations on where to eat and what to see in each location. It is lightweight, relatively water resistant, and measures 5 inches by 8.5 inches so that it fits in an outside pants or pack pocket. This is by far the most detailed.

Walking the Camino de Santiago, from St. Jean Pied de Port to Santiago de Compostella and on to Finisterre by Bethan Davies and Ben Cole

> This book has all of the same features as Brierley's book, but it is a little less detailed on the walking directions and places to stay. However, I liked the descriptions of the climate, geography, history, flaura and fauna, food, customs and culture of each

region better. It was more entertaining reading and gave me a better feeling for the countryside I would be passing through. It measures 8.5 inches by 5.5 inches.

Both of these books are excellent. Tannis and I took both books to share, and each of us carried one.

Art Materials

If you want to take art materials, the space inside your pack and the weight you can carry will be very limited. I chose a 9 inch by 12 inch Bee paper company professional series drawing pad with 60 sheets of heavyweight paper and a stiff cardboard cover. This provided a good surface for drawing that was durable and heavy enough to stand up to the journey in my pack without damage. I chose Micron Archival Ink pens made by Sakura that are waterproof and fade proof. I tested several brands of pens by writing on a sample of my sketchbook paper and holding them under running water. Some brands ran and bled, but the Micron was water fast and dried perfectly with no distortion. I took one each #1, #3, #5, and #8. This was sufficient for the entire trip, but I did have to purchase a few more to finish the drawings at home. I packed the sketchbook and pens in double zip-lock bags and kept them packed next to my back inside my backpack to prevent water damage.

Take only the size and number of sheets of paper that you think you will reasonably use. Paper is heavy, and in the big towns like Pamplona, Burgos, and Leon you can purchase more if necessary.

Colored pencils or colored ink pens (as long as they are waterproof!) also make a fine choice of media.

If you choose to take paints, think very carefully. You could take a small watercolor kit. However, I considered watercolor to be too fragile because the finished paintings would be damaged or ruined if accidentally exposed to the rain and other weather elements. Acrylics are more durable, but also add too much bulk and weight for a backpacking trip. I have tried this before, and it was not a success. Oil paints are out of the question due to the slow drying time.

Journal

I took a waterproof ballpoint pen and a Moleskine hardbacked journal, measuring 5 inches by 8 inches. The paper is waterproof and there were sufficient pages for my very long entries on the whole trip.

Purchase in Spain

The pharmacies in Spain have everything you need in the way of first aid and personal hygiene. When you need more shampoo, toothpaste, anti-inflammatory drugs, an ace bandage, suntan lotion, Compeed for blisters, cold remedies, etc., you can easily purchase them at reasonable prices in almost any town. We bought shampoo only one time, and after refilling our bottles, we passed it around to all the other pilgrims to do the same so that we did not need to carry a larger bottle. Do not overload your pack trying to plan for every eventuality, as it is simply not necessary. The pharmacies also act as consultants, giving you advice and over-the-counter medications that would require a doctor's visit in the U.S.

Also buy your pilgrim's scallop shell in Spain or France when you begin your journey.

Packing list

Clothes

    3 pairs underwear
    2 sports bras
    4 pairs socks
    3 fast-drying T-shirts
    1 pair silk boxer shorts (or something to sleep in)
    1 long-sleeve, lightweight travel shirt
    1 pair long travel pants
    1 pair Capri-length yoga pants or other comfortable walking pants
    1 travel-weight skirt
    1 waterproof and windproof jacket

1 long-sleeve fleece jacket with a full zip
1 pair rain pants
1 pair gloves
1 Buff or scarf
1 OR brand "wind stopper" ski hat
1 sun-blocking hat
1 pair hiking boots
1 pair alternate foot-bed liners for your boots
1 pair Crocs or other shoes/sandals

Acccessories

1 water bottle or hydration system
1 small nylon shoulder bag or daypack: count the ounces!
Sunglasses/ reading glasses/paper prescription
1 pair earplugs
1 small fast-drying travel towel
1 mini flashlight or headlight
1 small sewing kit with 3 or 4 safety pins
1 stretchy travel laundry line with 4-6 plastic clips and a sink plug
1 small clock or watch that you can read in the dark
1 pair nail clippers
1 pocketknife1 scallop shell: purchase in Spain or France

Toiletries/First Aid (See also "Purchase in Spain")

1 or 2 travel-size shampoo
1small soap
1 toothbrush
1 small toothpaste
Dental floss
2 hair bands or clips
1 small sunscreen for your face
1 razor
1 set tweezers
1 ChapStick
1 small bottle ibuprofen

Personal medications
A few Band-Aids

Other items
1 well-designed backpack
1 backpack rain cover
1 sleeping bag with waterproof stuff sack **or** sleep-sack for summer
1 pair trekking poles
1 "portable bathroom"
Several zip-lock plastic bags
1 journal and pen
1 camera, extra batteries, charger and plug adapter, extra memory chip
1 phone and charger
1 guidebook to the Camino

Optional for Artists
1 sketchbook
Pencil, pens, or a very tiny, lightweight painting setup with watercolor paper.

Organizing Your Pack

It can be frustrating to dig through everything in your pack and finally find the item you are looking for at the very bottom. My pack was so organized that a German man who was an engineer actually took a picture of it. I was so proud of my uber-organized German genes!

I used gallon zip-lock bags to sort everything into categories. Then I labeled them in bold lettering with a black marker. For example, the "sleep" bag contained everything I needed for bedtime: my T-shirt, shorts, earplugs, and clock. Each bag held only a few items, such as pants or underwear. When we arrived at our Albergue I could dump everything out on my bunk and quickly find what I needed. The items also stayed relatively wrinkle free, clean, and dry. I had a separate bag for dirty clothes, and one for wet clothes that may not have dried entirely the night before.

I placed my sleeping bag at the very bottom of the pack. Toiletries and towel went on top of the sleeping bag. My sketchbook and journal went into a second plastic bag and fit flat against my back. The clothes, shoes, and other miscellaneous things filled the rest of the main compartment.

The outside top compartment carried my jacket, rain pants, and pack cover. My money, credit card, and passport were separately bagged and tucked in the same compartment. The outside center section held my fleece jacket, hat, gloves, and food for the day. Both of these compartments were easily accessible if I took off my pack or if Tannis reached in for me. Putting these items on would have required removing my pack anyway.

The most easily accessible compartments were saved for things I needed to be able to reach as I went along. The outside lower compartments contained my sunglasses, ChapStick, Buff, portable bathroom, ibuprofen, water bottle, and on cool days, my gloves. My camera was clipped to my pack waist strap. My baseball cap was either on my head or hanging off the side of my pack by a clip.

However you organize your pack, try to think of what you will need along the way each day and keep it on the outside.

Sources

These first two also provide excellent information while on the walk, as explained in the above section, "Guidebooks to the Camino."

A Pilgrim's Guide to the Camino de Santiago , St. Jean Pied de Port-Santiago de Compostela, John Brierley

Walking the Camino de Santiago, from St. Jean Pied de Port to Santiago de Compostella and on to Finisterre, Bethan Davies and Ben Cole

These next two give useful information about the area and sights but do not belong in your pack, weighting you down on the path. Read them before you go, and refer to them again when you return home.

The Pilgrimage Road to Santiago, David M. Gitlitz and Linda Kay Davidson

Northern Spain, Cadogan guides, Dana Facaros and Michael Pauls

Rick Steves' Spain, Rick Steves

Jose and his song are on the Web at http://dailymotion.com, then go to ACOGENOS, then Miroperegrino.

WWOOF (World Wide Opportunities on Organic Farms): http://www.wwoof.org/

About the Author and Artist

Frequent moves throughout Oregon due to my father's job gave me the opportunity to develop my outgoing personality as well as to appreciate different environments and feel comfortable in any situation—the perfect background for traveling.

In contrast to constantly being uprooted from schools and homes, I had the stability of family and our ranches in northeastern Oregon. We spent every vacation and summer on them, tending to farm activities, working the cattle, and riding the wide-open range.

No wonder, then, that the land figures large in my paintings. I work in watercolor, acrylic, and oil and find each medium lends its own way of expressing my vision of the world. But all carry commonalities. My bold use of color reflects my cheerful and upbeat nature. And a strong sense of the graphic keeps my works grounded while my interpretive application brings out a spiritual connection.

I see the landscape as a metaphor for the lives we live and the mysterious spiritual forces constantly at work. It takes on human characteristics for me, and as I take note of the intricate beauty displayed, I merge with it, becoming one with all. As it struggles, so do I. As it changes, so do I. And as it embraces new life, so do I with joy unbounded.

I have been married to Craig Shaver since I was eighteen years old, and we have one son, Justin. Craig's three years in the US Navy in Asia gave me the opportunity to hone my traveling skills as I ventured to the Far East countries on my own, approaching others with respect and receiving the same—and more—in return. We returned to civilian life in the States where we completed our university education. I earned a Bachelor of Science degree from the University of Oregon in art education, with masters and travel studies in Europe and Asia, and taught art at the high school level. I furthered my art studies at the Gage Academy of Art in Seattle, graduating from the landscape atelier immersion program.

My prints and original paintings are featured in private and corporate collections internationally. A former president of Eastside Association of Fine Arts, I continue my twenty-plus years of active involvement in this organization that supports artists at all levels of development.

I have lived in Redmond, Washington, for the past thirty years and take full advantage of the beautiful world at our doorstep through boating, camping, water sports, snow skiing, hiking, and a variety of other outdoor activities as a family.

> Though we travel the world over to find the beautiful,
> we must carry it with us or we find it not.
>
> Ralph Waldo Emerson

Hold onto the beautiful. Carry it with you always. And share it with each person you meet.

To view Marcia's artwork, or purchase prints and books, visit her websites at:
www.marciashaver.com
www.theartistsjourney.com